CAMBRIDGE LIBRARY COLLECTION

Books of enduring scholarly value

Linguistics

From the earliest surviving glossaries and translations to nineteenth century academic philology and the growth of linguistics during the twentieth century, language has been the subject both of scholarly investigation and of practical handbooks produced for the upwardly mobile, as well as for travellers, traders, soldiers, missionaries and explorers. This collection will reissue a wide range of texts pertaining to language, including the work of Latin grammarians, groundbreaking early publications in Indo-European studies, accounts of indigenous languages, many of them now extinct, and texts by pioneering figures such as Jacob Grimm, Wilhelm von Humboldt and Ferdinand de Saussure.

A Handbook of Phonetics

As a phonetician and comparative philologist, Henry Sweet (1845–1912) produced work that was regarded as seminal, particularly in Germany, where he received greater academic recognition than in England. His text-books on Old English have long been considered standard works. As well as theoretical and historical studies, he also became involved in more practical aspects of linguistics, devising a new kind of shorthand, discussing spelling reform, and promoting the teaching and learning of modern languages. He played a role in the early history of the *Oxford English Dictionary* and edited several works for the Early English Text Society. Shaw's Professor Higgins in *Pygmalion* is believed to be based at least partly on Sweet. The present work, first published in 1877, inspired European interest in phonetic studies. Sweet presents a general theory of phonetics, illustrated by examples of transcription from various languages. He also formulates the distinction between phonemic and allophonic transcriptions.

Cambridge University Press has long been a pioneer in the reissuing of out-of-print titles from its own backlist, producing digital reprints of books that are still sought after by scholars and students but could not be reprinted economically using traditional technology. The Cambridge Library Collection extends this activity to a wider range of books which are still of importance to researchers and professionals, either for the source material they contain, or as landmarks in the history of their academic discipline.

Drawing from the world-renowned collections in the Cambridge University Library and other partner libraries, and guided by the advice of experts in each subject area, Cambridge University Press is using state-of-the-art scanning machines in its own Printing House to capture the content of each book selected for inclusion. The files are processed to give a consistently clear, crisp image, and the books finished to the high quality standard for which the Press is recognised around the world. The latest print-on-demand technology ensures that the books will remain available indefinitely, and that orders for single or multiple copies can quickly be supplied.

The Cambridge Library Collection brings back to life books of enduring scholarly value (including out-of-copyright works originally issued by other publishers) across a wide range of disciplines in the humanities and social sciences and in science and technology.

A Handbook of Phonetics

Including a Popular Exposition
of the Principles of Spelling Reform

HENRY SWEET

CAMBRIDGE
UNIVERSITY PRESS

CAMBRIDGE
UNIVERSITY PRESS

University Printing House, Cambridge, CB2 8BS, United Kingdom

Published in the United States of America by Cambridge University Press, New York

Cambridge University Press is part of the University of Cambridge.

It furthers the University's mission by disseminating knowledge in the pursuit of
education, learning and research at the highest international levels of excellence.

www.cambridge.org
Information on this title: www.cambridge.org/9781108062282

© in this compilation Cambridge University Press 2013

This edition first published 1877
This digitally printed version 2013

ISBN 978-1-108-06228-2 Paperback

Clarendon Press Series

HANDBOOK OF PHONETICS

SWEET

a

London

MACMILLAN AND CO.

PUBLISHERS TO THE UNIVERSITY OF

Oxford

Clarendon Press Series

A

HANDBOOK OF PHONETICS

INCLUDING A

POPULAR EXPOSITION OF

THE PRINCIPLES OF SPELLING REFORM

BY

HENRY SWEET

President of the Philological Society
Author of a 'History of English Sounds,' &c,

Oxford

AT THE CLARENDON PRESS

M DCCC LXXVII

PREFACE.

THE importance of phonetics as the indispensable foundation of all study of language—whether that study be purely theoretical, or practical as well—is now generally admitted. Without a knowledge of the laws of sound-change, scientific philology—whether comparative or historical—is impossible, and without phonetics their study degenerates into a mere mechanical enumeration of letter-changes. And now that philologists are directing their attention more and more to the study of living dialects and savage languages, many of which have to be written down for the first time, the absolute necessity of a thorough practical as well as theoretical mastery of phonetics becomes more and more evident. Many instances might be quoted of the way in which important philological facts and laws have been passed over or misrepresented through the observer's want of phonetic training [a]. Again, if our present wretched system of studying modern languages is ever to be reformed, it must be on the basis of a preliminary training in general phonetics, which would at the same time lay the foundation for a thorough practical study of the pronunciation

[a] Schleicher's failing to observe the Lithuanian accents, or even to comprehend them when pointed out by Kurschat, is a striking instance.

b

and elocution of our own language—subjects which are totally ignored in our present scheme of education.

Until within the last few years phonetics was hardly recognised as a science in this country, and it is to Germany that we owe the first attempt to construct a general system of sounds on a physiological basis— E. Brücke's *Grundzüge der Physiologie der Sprachlaute* (2nd ed., Wien, 1876). The investigation of the mechanism of the glottis in producing speech-sounds received a great impulse from the use of the laryngoscope, first introduced by Garcia, whose investigations were continued in Germany with brilliant success by Czermak, Merkel, and others. The latter, in his *Anthropophonik* (1856), and in the shorter and more convenient *Physiologie der menschlichen Sprache* (Leipzig, 1866), has accumulated a mass of details on the physiology of the vocal organs which for fulness and accuracy stands quite alone. The purely acoustic investigation of speech-sounds begun by Donders in Holland, and carried out more in detail by Helmholz in his celebrated work *Die Lehre von den Tonempfindungen* [a], seems likely to have a very important influence on the progress of phonetics. The main results of German investigation have lately been summed up in a most masterly manner and in a moderate compass by Ed. Sievers in his *Grundzüge der Lautphysiologie* (Leipzig, 1876), which has almost entirely superseded the older work of Brücke.

The fact that the majority of those who have worked at phonetics in Germany have been physiologists and physicists rather than practical linguists, naturally accounts

---

[a] Now accessible to the English reader in Mr. A. J. Ellis's translation.

both for the merits and the defects of the German school. German investigation of the mechanism of the throat-sounds and of the consonants is in most respects very full and satisfactory, while the treatment of the vowels is, even in the latest work of Sievers, utterly inadequate, the vowels being arranged according to their sound, without any regard to their formation, the result being that vowels which are formed by perfectly distinct mechanisms are confounded, only because they happen to be similar in sound. The confusion is made worse by the assumption that all vowel-sounds must necessarily fit in as intermediates between the supposed primitive vowels *a*, *i* and *u*, whence that unfortunate triangular arrangement of the vowels which has done so much to perpetuate error and prevent progress.

The results of German phonetic investigation were first popularised in England by Professor Max Müller in the second series of his well-known *Lectures on Language* (1864), who also made use of various essays by our countryman Mr. A. J. Ellis—the pioneer of scientific phonetics in England.

In 1867 Mr. M. A Bell's *Visible Speech* appeared. It is no exaggeration to say that Bell has in this work done more for phonetics than all his predecessors put together : it is at least certain that his system is the first which gives a really adequate and comprehensive view of the whole field of possible sounds. His analysis of the vowel-positions is almost entirely new and original. His system of notation, in which the mechanism of the sounds is most ingeniously symbolised, is not only founded on an adequate analysis, but is also thoroughly practical in character, providing forms not only for printing, but also for writing, both in long- and short-hand [a], applicable to all languages.

Mr. Ellis's great work on *Early English Pronunciation*, of which four thick volumes have been published since 1869, and which is still in progress, has not only inaugurated the scientific historical study of English pronunciation, but also contains an immense mass of specifically phonetic details, together with the results of German investigation, which were not accessible to Bell, and also those of other phonetic observers, among whom Prince L. L. Bonaparte takes a prominent position. One of Mr. Ellis's most important contributions to practical phonetics is his adaptation of the ordinary Roman alphabet for the accurate representation of minute shades of sound, which is effected without having recourse either to new types or to those diacritics which make such systems as the well-known 'General Alphabet' of Lepsius impracticable for ordinary use.

The result is that England may now boast a flourishing phonetic school of its own, among whose younger members may be mentioned Dr. J. A. Murray, Mr. H. Nicol, and myself. Mr. Ellis's dialectal researches have also brought to light many highly gifted phonetic students, among whom the names of Ellworthy, Hallam, and Goodchild at once suggest themselves.

As yet the results of Bell's investigations have made hardly any impression outside of England and America. The truth is that his 'Visible Speech' is too rigidly systematic and not explanatory enough to be readily understood without oral instruction. Naturally, too, it is not

---

[a] Bell's system of shorthand is described in his *Universal Phono-Stenography*.

perfect in all its details, and some of the key-words from foreign languages seem to be wrongly chosen [a]. Professor Storm, of Christiania, whose practical command of sounds will not easily be rivalled, and who has carefully studied the works of our English phoneticians, represented these defects very forcibly to me, and urged me to write an exposition of the main results of Bell's investigations, with such additions and alterations as would be required to bring the book up to the present state of knowledge. I only hope it may induce foreign students to turn their attention to English phonetic work more than they have hitherto done.

As regards my qualifications for the task, I may briefly state that I studied practically under Mr. Bell himself, discussing doubtful points with him, Mr. Ellis, and especially with my fellow-student Mr. H. Nicol, and since then have been engaged almost without intermission in the practical study of foreign pronunciations, and have not only carefully read the best works of foreign phoneticians, but have also had the advantage of hearing the pronunciation of many of the writers themselves.

In order to make my statements as trustworthy as possible, I have, as far as possible, followed Sievers' excellent rule of only adducing sounds that I have heard myself. Most of the sounds described in this book occur in languages which I have studied grammatically in detail, several of them in the countries themselves, though mostly for very short periods.

The chief points in which I differ from Bell are the

[a] Thus he identifies French *u* with my (ə)—the mid instead of the high vowel—and French close *eu* with the wide (ə), and analyses the German *ei* as (ehi).

following :—his analysis of (th) and (dh), and of (f) and
(v), which last he considers to be divided consonants;
his 'glide'-theory; his theory of syllabification, and
his synthesis generally, which I consider inadequate.
Lastly in many questions of detail, such as his voiceless
(l) in *felt*, his unaccented vowels in English, and several
of his identifications of foreign sounds.

Although my work has mainly been that of summa-
rising and criticising the investigations of others, I have
been able to add some original results of my own.   Thus
I have tried to analyse Bell's distinction of 'primary'
and 'wide' more accurately, and have shown that it
applies to consonants, and not, as Bell assumed, to
vowels only.   Many of my views on the details of synthesis are, to some extent at least, original, especially the
analysis and classification of diphthongs, the varieties of
breathed and voiced stops, and syllabification.   The complete separation of Synthesis from Analysis was mainly
suggested by the arrangement followed by Sievers.   Many
of the analyses and identifications of special sounds are
also new.

It need hardly be said that many of the statements
in this book—whether the result of my predecessors' or
my own researches—will require careful examination by
others before they can be either fully received or rejected.
The whole subject of intonation, especially, requires to
be thoroughly investigated by a thoroughly competent
observer, which I am very far from being, my natural
aptitude and my training being equally defective.   It is
in this branch, in the study of voice-timbre and of synthesis generally, that the work of future phoneticians must
be concentrated.

The notation I have adopted is, like Mr. Ellis's 'Palæotype,' based on the ordinary Roman letters, which I have tried to employ more consistently than Mr. Ellis has done, by utilising the results of his manifold experiments and practical experience.

I have in most cases retained Bell's terminology, which is admirably clear and concise. Besides the necessary modifications in the names of special sounds I have ventured to substitute ' narrow' for his ' primary,' and to discard the term ' mixed' in describing the compound consonants, substituting, for instance, ' lip-back' for the vaguer ' lip-mixed,' and, lastly, to coin the new term ' blade.'

As this book is intended mainly to serve practical purposes, I have not attempted to go into the details of physiology, anatomy, or acoustics, for which I must refer to the works of Merkel, Helmholz, &c. Merkel's works also contain excellent drawings of the different organs and their actions. I have not ventured on any diagrams of the vowel-positions, and can only refer the reader to those in ' Visible Speech ᵃ,' merely remarking that those of (e) and (æ) do not allow enough distance between the tongue and the palate, and that that of the consonant (th) is, as Mr. Bell himself confessed to me, misleading.

The specimens will, I hope, prove useful in several ways. They are written as accurately as possible, so as to show the real synthesis of the languages, and are not

---

ᵃ Those who have not the larger work should procure the shilling pamphlet *Visible Speech for the Million* (Trübner), which contains the same diagrams and symbols together with a general sketch of the system.

patched together, as is too often the case, by joining
words together in the artificial pronunciation of the pronouncing dictionaries. I feel painfully that many of these
specimens urgently require revision. The difficulty is,
that what seems an adequate analysis at a given time
may be quite inadequate a year after, because of the pro-
gressiveness inseparable from a young science. My study
of Icelandic pronunciation, for instance, was made nearly
ten years ago, when I first began 'Visible Speech,' but
adverse circumstances have prevented me from revising
it properly since, and I can only hope that the imperfections of my phonetic knowledge at that time were compensated by the advantage of having acquired the sounds
while still young.

The Appendix on Spelling Reform will I trust be not
unacceptable to those who wish to acquire a general
knowledge of the main facts and principles involved in
the question, without being obliged to go into the minutiæ
of phonetic science. It may also prove useful to travellers, missionaries and others, who wish for some aid in
writing the sounds of unwritten dialects or savage languages.

The proper way of studying phonetics is, of course,
to go through a regular course under a competent teacher,
for phonetics can no more be acquired by mere reading
than music can. Those who have no teacher must begin
with carefully analysing their own natural pronunciation,
until they have some idea of its relation to the general
scale of sounds. They can then proceed to deduce the
pronunciation of unfamiliar sounds from their relations
to known sounds (§ 51), checking the results by a practical study of the languages in which the new sounds

occur. A thorough study of French pronunciation under a native will do more than anything to free the student from one-sided English associations and habits. Nor let him delude himself with the idea that he has already acquired French pronunciation at school or elsewhere: in nine cases out of ten a little methodical study of sounds will convince him that he does not pronounce a single French sound correctly.

The student should not allow himself to be disheartened by the slowness of his progress and the obtuseness of his ear, for even the most highly gifted and best trained are often baffled for weeks and even months by some sound which another will find quite easy both to distinguish by ear and to pronounce. A great deal depends on the character of the native language, the learner naturally grafting the peculiarities of his own language on his pronunciation of foreign ones, as when an Englishman diphthongises the long vowels in French and German; and, again, finding those sounds difficult which do not occur, or have no analogues, in his own pronunciation. It is a great mistake to suppose that any one nation has a special gift for acquiring sounds or foreign languages generally. Each nation has its special defects or advantages. The Russian pronunciation of German, for instance, is at once betrayed by the substitution of (ih) for the *ü* and by many other peculiarities : in fact, those Russians and Poles who speak French and German perfectly are often unable to speak their own languages properly. The more civilised and influential a nation is the worse linguists are those who speak its language ; but when Englishmen (and even Frenchmen) really devote themselves to the practical study of language, they prove

quite equal to other nations, as, for instance, Dutchmen
or Russians, who are obliged, the former by the small-
ness of their country, the latter by their barbarism, to
learn a number of foreign languages. It cannot, of course,
be denied that some languages are a worse preparation
for the acquisition of foreign sounds than others, but a
thorough training in general phonetics soon levels the
inequality, and enables the learner to develope his special
gifts independently of outward circumstances. It is on
its value as the foundation of the practical study of language that the claims of phonetics to be considered an
essential branch of education mainly rest.

Christiania, Aug. 27, 1877.

LIST OF THE MORE IMPORTANT SYMBOLS
EMPLOYED IN THIS WORK.

N.B.   *The turned letters follow immediately after the unturned.*

a . . . . father.

ɐ . . . . but.

a . . . . *broad* (a).

ɒ . . . . *broad* (ɐ).

$\left.\begin{array}{l} \text{A} \\ \text{v} \end{array}\right\}$ . . *varieties of* (ɐ).

æ . . . men (*open* e).

ӕ . . . man.

æh . . . turn.

ӕh . . . *opener* (æh).

b . . . . bee.

bh . . . *German* w.

bh*j* . . *palatalised* (bh).

(ɔ *after* o).

d . . . . day.

dh . . . then.

dh*j* . . *palatalised* (dh).

ᴅ . . . . *palatal* (d).

e . . . . *close* e.

ə . . . . *French close* eu.

e . . . . *variety of open* e.

ɵ . . . . *variety of French open* eu.

$\left.\begin{array}{l} \text{eh} \\ \text{eh} \end{array}\right\}$ . . *German unaccented* e.

f . . . . fee.

g . . . . go.

gh . . . *voiced* (kh).

gh*r* . . *trilled* (gh).

gh*w* . . *labialised* (gh).

$\left.\begin{array}{l} \text{g}j \\ \text{G} \end{array}\right\}$ = *palatalised* (g).

h . . $\left\{\begin{array}{l} \textit{general diacritic.} \\ \quad \textit{Initially for} (\textsc{h}). \end{array}\right.$

ʜ . . . *aspirate.*

ʜh . . . *open glottis.*

i . . . . *narrow* i.

ɩ . . . . *wide* i.

ih . . . *Welsh* u.

ɩh . . . *wide* (ih).

j . . . . you.

jh . . . *voiceless* (j).

jh*w* . . *labialised* (jh).

kh . . . *Scotch* ch.

kh*r* . . *trilled* (kh).

kh*w* . . *labialised* (kh).

kʜ . . . *aspirated* (k).

$\left.\begin{array}{l} \text{k}j \\ \text{K} \end{array}\right\}$ . . *palatalised* (k).

l . . . . lee

lh . . . *voiceless* (l).

L	. . . *palatal* (l).	Rh	. . *voiceless* (R).
ꞁ	. . . *guttural* (l).	s	. . . *say.*
m	. . . *may.*	s*j*	. . . *palatalised* (s).
mh	. . *voiceless* (m).	sh	. . . *fish.*
n	. . . *now.*	sh*j*	. . *palatalised* (sh).
nh	. . *voiceless* (n).	sh*w*	. . *labialised* (sh).
n	. . . *nasality.*	t	. . . *tea.*
N	. . . *palatal* (n).	th	. . . *thing.*
o	. . . *close* o.	th*j*	. . . *palatalised* (th).
o	. . . *open* o.	tH	. . . *aspirated* (t).
oh	. . . *between* (o) *and* (ə).	T	. . . *palatal* (t).
oh	. . . *between* (*o*) *and* (*ɔ*).	u	. . . *narrow* u.
ɔ	. . . *open* o *in* all.	uh	. . . *Swedish* u.
ɔh	. . . *between* (ɔ) *and* (œ).	*u*	. . . *wide* (*English*) u.
ɔ	. . . *open* o *in* not.	*uh*	. . . *wide* (uh).
ɔh	. . . *between* (*ɔ*) *and* (œ).	v	. . . *vie.*
œ	. . . *open French* eu.	ʌ	. . . *voice.*
œ	. . . *wide* (œ).	ʌh ⎫	. *whisper.*
p	. . . *pay.*	ʻʌ ⎭	
ph	. . . *voiceless* (bh).	w	. . . *we.*
ph*j*	. . *palatalised* (ph).	wh	. . *why.*
pH	. . . *aspirated* (p).	*w*	. . . *labialisation.*
q	. . . *sing.*	x	. . . *glottal catch.*
qh	. . . *voiceless* (q).	y	. . . *French* u.
q	. . . *French nasality.*	*y*	. . . *wide* (y).
r	. . . *red.*	z	. . . *zeal.*
r	. . . *trilled.*	zh	. . . *rouge.*
r*r*	. . . *trilled* (r).		
rh	. . . *voiceless* (r).	(a)ɪ	. . . *length.*
rh*r*	. . *trilled* (rh).	aɪɪ	. . . *extra length.*
r*j*	. . . *palatalised* (r).	a·	. . . *stress* (*force*).
R	. . . *laryngal* r.	a··	. . . *extra stress.*

a: . . . *half stress.*

ā̈ . . . *level*

ā̆ . . . *increasing* $\Big\}$ *force.*

ā̃ . . . *diminishing*

— . . . *level*

∕ . . . *rising*

∖ . . . *falling* $\Big\}$ *tone.*

∨ . . . *falling and rising*

∧ . . . *rising and falling*

[i] . . . *glide.*

'z . . . *whispered* (s), &c.

a̦ . . . *inner* (away from the teeth).

a̧ . . . *outer.*

r⊥ . . . *inverted* (*cerebral*).

r† . . . *protruded.*

* . . . *simultaneity of the two sounds it comes between.*

e¹ . . . *raised tongue.*

o¹ . . . *narrowed lip-opening.*

CONTENTS.

PART I.

THE ORGANS OF SPEECH.

1. The foundation of speech is breath expelled by the lungs and variously modified in the throat and mouth [a].

2. The breath passes from the lungs through the windpipe into the larynx ('Adam's apple'). Across the interior of the larynx are stretched two elastic ligaments, the 'vocal chords.' They are firmly inserted in the front of the larynx at one end, while at the other they are fixed to two movable cartilaginous bodies, the 'arytenoids,' so that the space between them, the 'glottis,' can be narrowed or closed at pleasure. The glottis is, as we see, twofold, consisting of the chord glottis, or glottis proper, and the cartilage glottis. The two glottises can be narrowed or closed independently. The chords can also be lengthened or shortened, tightened or relaxed in various degrees by means of the muscles they contain.

3. Above the 'true' glottis, and still forming part of the larynx, comes the 'upper' or 'false' glottis, by which the passage can be narrowed or partially closed. On the top of the larynx is fixed a sort of valve, the 'epiglottis,' which in swallowing and in the formation of certain

[a] The exceptions to this general definition are very few. The most important are the 'clicks' (§ 176, below).

sounds is pressed down so as to cover the opening of the larynx.

4. The cavity between the larynx and the mouth is called the 'pharynx.' It can be expanded and contracted in various ways.

5. The roof of the mouth consists of two parts, the soft and the hard palate. The lower pendulous extremity of the soft palate, the 'uvula,' can be pressed backwards or forwards. It is pressed back in closing the passage into the nose. When the pressure is relaxed, as in ordinary breathing without speech, the breath flows through the nose as well as the mouth.

6. The other extremity of the palate is bounded by the teeth, of which we must distinguish the 'edges' and the 'rim,' or place where they join the gums. The gums extend from the teeth-rim to the 'arch-rim,' behind which comes the 'arch,' whose front wall is formed by the 'teeth roots' (alveolars).

7. Of the tongue we distinguish the 'back,' the middle or 'front,' and the tip or 'point,' together with the 'blade,' which includes the upper surface of the tongue immediately behind the point. 'Lower blade' implies, of course, the lower, instead of the upper surface.

8. Besides the main positions indicated by these names, an indefinite number of intermediate ones are possible. The chief varieties are designated by the terms 'inner' and 'outer,' inner implying nearer the back of the mouth, outer nearer the teeth. Thus the 'outer front' of the tongue is a place nearer the point than simple front, and is therefore an approximation to the 'blade.'

Sounds are also modified by the degree of separation of the jaws, and by the movements of the lips and cheeks.

PART II.

ANALYSIS.

—◈—

THROAT SOUNDS.

BREATH, VOICE, AND WHISPER.

9. When the glottis is wide open, no sound is produced by the outgoing breath, except that caused by the friction of the air in the throat, mouth, &c. This passive state of the glottis is called 'breath' (ʜh) [a].

10. The most important 'active' states of the glottis are those which produce 'voice' and 'whisper.'

11. Voice (ʌ) [b] is produced by the action of the breath on the vocal chords in two ways. (1) If the glottis is entirely closed by the chords so that the air can only pass through in a series of puffs, we have that most sonorous form of voice known as the 'chest' voice or 'thick register' of the voice. (2) If the chords are only brought close enough together to enable their edges to vibrate, without any closure of the glottis, that thinner quality of voice known as the 'head' voice or 'thin register' is produced, which in its thinnest and shrillest form is called 'falsetto.'

---

[a] The usual diacritic (') *before* the modified letter is also occasionally employed to denote breath. See §§ 12 and 16.

[b] (ʌ), = turned v, = 'voice.'

B 2

12. If the chords are approximated without being allowed to vibrate, whisper (ʌh), ('ʌ), is produced. There are two degrees of whisper, the 'weak' and the 'medium.' In the weak whisper the whole glottis is narrowed; in the medium, which is the ordinary form, the chord glottis is entirely closed, so that the breath passes only through the cartilage glottis.

13. The distinctions of breath, voice, and whisper are the most general of all, for every sound must be uttered with the glottis either open, narrowed, or closed, and the same sound may be pronounced either breathed, voiced, or whispered. Thus, if we press the lower lip against the upper teeth edges, we have the position of the 'lip-teeth' consonant. If we drive the air from the lungs through the passage thus formed, leaving the glottis open, we obtain the 'lip-teeth breath' consonant (f). If the chords are narrowed till voice is produced, we obtain the 'lip-teeth voice' consonant (v). If the student prolongs an (f), and then a (v), without any vowel, he will soon see that in the case of (f) the sound is formed entirely in the teeth, while with (v) the sound is distinctly compound, the hiss in the teeth being accompanied by a murmur in the throat. If he presses his two first fingers firmly on the glottis, he will distinctly feel a vibration in the case of (v), but not of (f). There is the same distinction between (s) and (z), (th) as in 'thin,' and (dh) as in 'then.'

14. It is of great importance to acquire a clear feeling of the distinction between breath and voice, and the student should accustom himself to sound all consonants both with and without voice at will. Such exercises as the following are very useful.

(1) Breathe strongly through the open glottis, and bring

the lips and teeth together, concentrating the attention as much as possible on the actions by which the sound, (f), is produced rather than on the sound itself.

(2) Make a vocal murmur, as in the word 'err,' and then bring the lips and teeth together as before, which produces (v).

(3) Prolong (f) and remove the lips from the teeth: the result will be simple breath, (нh).

(4) Repeat the process with (v), and the result will be simple voice (ʌ).

(5) Pass without stopping from (f) to (s), (th), and (sh), and from (v) to (z), (dh), and (zh) as in 'rouge,' observing the unchanged state of the glottis while the lips and tongue shift continually.

(6) Pass without stopping from (f) to (v) and from (v) to (f), and so with the other consonants, observing the change in the glottis while the organic positions remain unchanged.

(7) Try to form from the familiar (l), (r), (n), (m) the unfamiliar breathed (lh), (rh), (nh), (mh).

15. The popular and the phonetic use of the term 'whisper' do not quite agree. Whisper in popular language simply means speech without voice. Phonetically speaking whisper implies not merely absence of voice, but a definite contraction of the glottis.

16. In ordinary whispering, as opposed to loud speech, what happens is this. Breathed elements, being already voiceless, remain unchanged. Voiced elements substitute whisper (in the phonetic sense) for voice. If we pronounce two such syllables as 'vee' and 'fee,' first in an ordinary loud voice and then in a whisper, we shall find that in 'vee' both consonant and vowel are changed, while in 'fee' only the vowel is changed, the consonant remaining breathed as in loud speech. It must, therefore, be understood in phonetic discussions that whenever we talk of a whispered sound we mean one that is pronounced with a definite contraction of the glottis. Whether we talk of a ' whispered (f)' or a ' whispered (v)' is indifferent— both names signify the 'lip-teeth whisper' consonant ('v)[a].

17. The acoustic distinction between breath and whisper is not very marked, but if we compare ('v) with (f), we perceive clearly that ('v) is, like (v), a composite sound, with a distinct friction in the larynx. Whispered sounds are also feebler than breath ones, the force of the outgoing air being diminished by the glottis contraction.

OTHER LARYNX SOUNDS.

18. *Glottal Catch* (x). When the glottis is suddenly opened or closed on a passage of breath or voice, a per-cussive effect is produced, analogous to that of (k) or any other ' stopped' consonant. The most familiar example of this ' glottal catch' is an ordinary cough. The student should carefully practise the glottal catch in combination with vowels till he is able to produce (xa) and (ax) as easily as (ka) and (ak), taking care not to let any breath escape after the (x) in (xa), as is the case in coughing. He should then learn to shut and open the glottis silently, and to know by the muscular sensation alone whether it is open or shut. It is easy to test the closure of the glottis by tapping on the throat above the larynx, which, when

---

[a] The ('),='breath,' combined with (v), which implies voice, suggests something intermediate to breath and voice, which is whisper. See Ellis, E. E. P. p. 1129.

the glottis is open, produces a dull sound, when shut, a clear and hollow one like the gurgling of water being poured into a bottle, and its pitch can be raised or lowered at pleasure by retracting or advancing the tongue.

19. (x) forms an essential element of some languages. It is common in Danish after vowels, and often distinguishes words which would otherwise be identical. Thus *hun* (hu'n) is 'she,' but *hund* (hux'n) is 'dog,' (kʜɔ'm) is 'come,' (kʜɔx'm) is 'came,' both written *kom*. According to Mr. Bell it is used in the Glasgow pronunciation of Scotch as a substitute for the voiceless stops, as in (waxehr*r*) ='water,' (bᴇxehr*r*)='butter.'

20. *Wheeze* (ʀh). If we strongly exaggerate an ordinary whisper, we produce that hoarse, wheezy sound known as the 'stage whisper.' In the formation of this sound there is not only the glottis narrowing of the ordinary medium whisper, but there is also contraction of the superglottal passage or 'false glottis,' the opening being further narrowed by depression of the epiglottis. The sound is a common variety of (r), especially when it is voiced (ʀ). It is the regular sound in Danish, the laryngal action being combined with retraction of the tongue and rounding, so that the sound is really (ʀ+gh*w*). (ʀ+gh) may also be heard in North Germany. If there is 'trilling' or vibration of the upper part of the glottis, the Arabic *Hha* (ʀh*r*) and *Ain* (ʀ*r*) are formed.

NASAL SOUNDS.

21. In ordinary breathing the uvula hangs loosely down, and the air passes behind it through the nose as well as the mouth. In forming all the non-nasal sounds the uvula is pressed up so as to cover the passage into the nose. If the passage is open the sound becomes nasal. Thus (b) and (m) are formed in exactly the same way except that with (b) the nasal passage is closed, with (m) it is open. Similarly, if in pronouncing the vowel (a) the uvula is lowered, we obtain the corresponding nasal vowel (a*n*).

22. The pure nasal vowels, which are common in many South German dialects, must be carefully distinguished from the French nasals, in which there is guttural compression as well as nasality, a combination which may be denoted by (q), thus (aq) is the French 'en,' 'an,' (oq) ='on,' (v$æq$)='vin,' (œq)='un'[a].

23. There are various degrees of nasality, according as the nose passage is completely or only partially open. Many speakers pronounce all their vowels with imperfect closure of the nose passage, which gives their pronunciation the so-called nasal twang.' This nasality is so common in North America, especially in New England, as to constitute a characteristic feature of American pronunciation. It is, however, very frequent in London English also.

NARROW AND WIDE.

24. These are very important general modifications of all sounds produced or modified in the mouth. They depend on the *shape* of the tongue. In forming narrow

---

[a] The exact formation of the French nasals has long been a disputed question. The guttural element I believe to be some kind of lateral cheek (and, perhaps, pharynx) compression: it is somewhat vaguely described by Mr. Bell as consisting in a 'semi-consonant contraction of the guttural passage.'

sounds there is a feeling of tenseness in that part of the
tongue where the sound is formed, the surface of the
tongue being made more convex than in its natural 'wide'
shape, in which it is relaxed and flattened. This convexity of the tongue naturally narrows the passage—whence
the name. This narrowing is produced by raising, not
the whole body of the tongue, but only that part of it
which forms, or helps to form, the sound. Thus, starting
from the mid-wide vowel (*e*) we may narrow the passage
either by raising the whole body of the tongue to the high
(*i*) position, or else by contracting the muscles in the
front of the tongue so as to make it more convex, without
otherwise changing its height. We may then raise this
narrow-mid (e) to the high (i) position. Although in (i)
the tongue is nearer the palate than in the wide (*i*), we can
never change (*i*) into (i) by simply raising the tongue :
we must alter its shape at the same time from wide to
narrow. If (*i*) is raised so high as to produce a distinct
consonantal hiss, it will still remain wide in sound.

25. The distinction of narrow and wide applies to consonants, and not (as Mr. Bell assumed) to vowels only.
The distinction between French and English (w) in 'oui'
and 'we' is that the French (w) is narrow, the English
wide, the former being consonantized (u), the latter (*u*).
In English the hisses are generally wide, in French narrow. Narrow (s) may be heard in energetic hissing, wide
(sh) in gentle hushing [a].

[a] Mr. Bell, who first noticed the distinction of narrow and wide,
explains it as due to tension and relaxation of the pharynx. I for a
long time held to this view, imagining the tension of the tongue to
be something secondary and merely sympathetic. However I afterwards noticed that the sense of pharyngal and palatal tension was
always concentrated on that part of the mouth where the sound was

26. The distinction being a delicate one is not to be acquired practically without considerable training. Beginners are apt to confuse widening with lowering of the tongue, especially when the wide vowel is unfamiliar. The best way to avoid this is to run through a whole series from high to low, first narrow and then wide, taking, for instance, first (i, e, æ), then (*i, e, æ*). In this way a clear idea of the distinction between changes in the *shape* and in the *position* of the tongue will be obtained.

27. A narrow vowel may be widened by trying to utter it as lazily and listlessly as possible, without altering the position of the tongue [a].

VOWELS.

28. A vowel may be defined as voice (voiced breath) modified by some definite configuration of the super-glottal passages, but without audible friction [b].

29. *Tongue Shape : Narrow and Wide.* The most important general modifications are those which cause the distinction of narrow and wide, already described. Wide

formed, in front sounds on the hard palate. This was a reductio ad absurdum, showing that the feeling was really imaginary. The relation was thus reversed : the tongue tension was shown to be the real cause of narrowness and wideness, and the other feeling to be imaginary and secondary. I do not believe that the shape of the pharynx, the approximation of the palatal arches, &c., have any effect in producing distinctive vowel sounds.

[a] Mr. Bell told me that he tried this method with success in teaching Frenchmen the English (*i*) and (*u*).

[b] *Whispered* vowels occur as integral elements of ordinary loud speech in some native American languages. See Haldeman, quoted by Ellis, E. E. P. p. 1194.

vowels are generally denoted by italics, thus (*i*) is the wide form of (i).

30. *Tongue Positions.* As each new position of the tongue produces a new vowel, and as the positions are infinite, it follows that the number of possible vowel sounds is infinite. It becomes necessary, therefore, to select certain definite positions as fixed points whence to measure the intermediate positions.

31. The movements of the tongue may be distinguished generally as horizontal and vertical—backwards and forwards, upwards and downwards. The horizontal movements produce two well-marked classes, (1) 'back' (guttural) vowels, in which the tongue is retracted as much as possible, such as (aɪ) in 'father,' (uɪ) in 'fool'; and (2) 'front' (palatal) vowels, such as (iɪ) in ' see,' (æ) in 'man,' in which the tongue is advanced. The former are formed by the back of the tongue only, the point being kept down, the latter by the front. The distinction is easily felt by pronouncing (aɪ) and (iɪ) in succession. There is also a third class, the ' mixed' (gutturo-palatal) vowels, which have an intermediate position, such as the English (æhɪ) in ' err,' the German (eh) in 'gabe.' Mixed vowels are indicated by the diacritical (h).

32. The vertical movements of the tongue produce various degrees of 'height,' or distance from the palate. Thus in (*i*), as in ' bit,' the front of the tongue is raised as high and as close to the palate as possible without causing friction, in (æ), as in ' man,' it is lowered as much as possible. From among the infinite degrees of height three are selected, ' high,' ' mid,' and ' low.' (*i*) is a high, (æ) a low vowel, while (*e*) as in ' say ' is a mid vowel. These distinctions apply equally to back, mixed, and

front vowels, so we have altogether nine cardinal vowel
positions :

high-back	high-mixed	high-front
mid-back	mid-mixed	mid-front
low-back	low-mixed	low-front

Each of these positions yields a different vowel sound
according as the tongue is in the 'narrow' or 'wide'
shape.

33. It is found that these nine positions correspond
very nearly with the actual distinctions made in language,
and that if we admit two intermediate positions between
each of them, we practically reach the limit of discrimination by ear. The intermediate heights are distinguished
as 'lowered' and 'raised,' thus the 'lowered high-front'
has a position below the 'high-front,' and above the 'raised
mid-front,' which is above the simple 'mid-front.'
Practically, however, the distinction between 'raised' and
'lowered' can hardly be carried out, and raised (e) and
lowered (i) must generally both be assumed to represent
the same half-way position. These vowels are written
thus, [ei]. Or exponents may be used, whenever accessible, (e¹). Horizontal intermediates are defined as
'inner' and 'outer,' and are indicated thus, (,e), (,eh), both
indicating practically the same sound. The student
should at first neglect these minutiæ, and concentrate his
attention on the elementary positions.

34. The height of the tongue is partly due to the
action of the muscles of the tongue itself, but also in a
great degree to the movements of the jaw. Thus if we
start from the high (i) position and lower the jaw,
allowing the tongue to sink with it, we obtain first the mid

(*e*) position and then the low (*æ*) one. Hence the partial closure of the mouth in forming high vowels.

35. The question naturally arises, Which of the nine positions is the natural one when the organs are at rest? If we vocalise the breath as emitted in ordinary quiet breathing, without shifting the tongue in any way, we obtain an indistinct nasal murmur, which, if de-nasalized by closure of the nose passage, resolves itself into the mid-mixed (or the low-mixed vowel, if the mouth is opened as wide as possible). We see, then, that the two 'natural' or 'neutral' vowels are (eh) and (*e*h), both of which are widely distributed in actual language.

36. *Rounding.* Rounding is a contraction of the mouth cavity by lateral compression of the cheek passage and narrowing of the lip aperture, whence the older name of 'labialization[a].' There are three principal degrees of lip-narrowing, corresponding to the height of the tongue, high vowels having the narrowest, low the widest lip-aperture. This is easily seen by comparing the high-back-round (uɪ), as in 'who,' the mid-back-round (oɪ), as in 'no,' and the low-back-round (ɔɪ), as in 'law.' It will be seen that in (uɪ) the lips are contracted to a narrow chink, while in (oɪ) the opening is wider and broader, and in (ɔɪ) only the corners of the mouth are contracted.

37. It will be observed that the action of rounding is always concentrated on that part of the mouth where the vowel is formed. In rounding front vowels, such as the high-front-round (y), as in the French 'lune,' the cheek compression is concentrated chiefly on the corners of the

[a] Mr. Bell says that 'the mechanical cause of round quality commences in the superglottal passage.' I find, however, that this is not essential.

mouth and that part of the cheeks immediately behind them, while in back vowels, such as the high-back-round (u) the chief compression is at the back of the cheeks.

38. Lip-narrowing is, therefore, something secondary in back-rounded vowels, as it is possible to form them entirely with cheek-narrowing or 'inner rounding.' The absence of lip-rounding is, however, distinctly perceptible. According to Mr. Bell inner rounding is practised by ventriloquists as a means of concealing the visible action of ordinary rounding.

39. The effect of rounding may, on the other hand, be increased by projecting (pouting) the lips, which of course practically lengthens the mouth channel by adding a resonance-chamber beyond the teeth. This action is generally avoided in English, but may often be observed in the Scotch (u), and generally in continental pronunciation.

40. The influence of the lips may also be observed in the unrounded vowels. In the formation of the low and mid vowels, such as (a), the lips are in the 'neutral' position of rest, but in forming the high (i) the mouth is spread out at the corners, which makes the sound of the vowel clearer [a]. This lip-spreading may, of course, be applied to (a) and the other vowels as well. It may also be neglected elsewhere, as is frequently the case in English, which dulls the effect of the high vowels.

41. If back vowels are pronounced with lip-narrowing alone (without inner rounding as well) we do not obtain the corresponding round vowels, but simply muffled

---

[a] I had not noticed this till I read the remarks of Sievers (L. Ph. p. 39).

varieties of the ordinary sounds. Similarly, if a front vowel is pronounced with inner rounding only, the result is simply a muffled, gutturalised front vowel, not a front rounded vowel [a].

42. Although there is a natural connection between the height of the tongue and the degree of lip-narrowing [b], there are cases of abnormal degrees of rounding in language. Thus in Danish and Swedish (o), as in ' sol,' always has the same lip-narrowing as (u), and (ɔ) as in ' maane,' ' måne,' has that of (o), the lip-narrowing being thus in each case a degree above the height of the tongue. Every vowel, whether narrow or wide, is capable of rounding, which gives a total of thirty-six elementary vowel-sounds.

TABLE OF VOWELS AND GENERAL REMARKS.

43. The thirty-six elementary vowels are given in the annexed table. Whenever an unambiguous key-word could be given from any of the better known languages, it has been added, especially from English (E.), Scotch (Sc.), French (F.), and German (G.). The English sounds are those of the educated southern pronunciation, the Scotch those of the Edinburgh pronunciation, and the German are distinguished as North (Hanoverian) German (N. G.), Middle (M.), and South (S.) German : ' occ.' signifies occasional.

---

[a] Cp. § 37.

[b] It would evidently be a waste of sound to narrow the back of the mouth and then allow the sound to diffuse itself in the front of the mouth, or to widen the back part of the channel and then muffle the sound by over-narrowing of the mouth channel.

GENERAL TABLE OF VOWELS.

NARROW.

	high-back	high-mixed	high-front
high	ɥ high-back	ih high-mixed N. Welsh tag*u*	i high-front F. fi*ni*
mid	ɐ mid-back E. b*u*t	eh mid-mixed G. gab*e*	e mid-front F. *été*
low	ɒ low-back Occ. Sc. b*u*t	æh low-mixed E. bi*r*d	æ low-front E. *air*

WIDE.

	high-back	high-mixed	high-front
high	ʌ high-back	ɪh high-mixed Occ. E. pretty	ɪ high-front E. bit
mid	ɑ mid-back E. father	eh mid-mixed E. eye (eh[ih])	e mid-front Danish træ
low	a low-back Sc. father	æh low-mixed E. how (æh[oh])	æ low-front E. man.

NARROW-ROUND.

	high-back	high-mixed	high-front
high	u high-back F. s*ou*	uh high-mixed Swedish h*us*	y high-front F. l*u*ne
mid	o mid-back G. s*o*	oh mid-mixed	ø mid-front F. p*eu*
low	ɔ low-back E. s*aw*	oh low-mixed	œ low-front F. p*eur*

WIDE-ROUND.

	high-back	high-mixed	high-front
high	u high-back E. full	uh high-mixed Swedish *u*pp	y high-front G. schützen
mid	o mid-back N. G. stock	oh mid-mixed F. homme	ø mid-front N. G. schön
low	o low-back E. not	oh low-mixed	œ low-front

44. *Names.* In naming the vowels, 'height' comes first, and 'rounding' last — 'high-back-narrow-round,' &c.

45. As regards the notation it may be remarked that all mixed vowels are indicated by adding the letter (h) in the case of unrounded mixed vowels to the corresponding front, in that of rounded mixed vowels to the corresponding back vowel symbol. Wide vowels are generally indicated by italics. The only exception is in the case of the back unrounded vowels, where the italics indicate widening of the mouth channel, not by relaxing, but by lowering the tongue. The narrow back unrounded vowels are indicated by the 'turned' letters of the corresponding wides. The relations of the front rounded and unrounded vowels are suggested by (ə), being a turned (e), and by the analogy of (œ) to (æ). (ɔ) is assumed to be a turned (o).

46. The relations of the symbols should be studied till they become perfectly familiar. The student should be able to answer at once such questions as the following. If (y) is unrounded, what is the result? What is the round vowel corresponding to (i)? If (o) is unrounded and widened, or if (a) is rounded and narrowed, what is the result?

47. *Practical Mastery of the Vowels.* While studying the symbols, the student should begin to acquire a practical mastery of the sounds themselves. This can only be done very gradually, beginning with those sounds which are perfectly familiar. One or two sounds should be taken at a time and repeated incessantly, till their mechanism is clearly felt and understood. Whispering the vowels will be found a great help in analysing their

c

formation. After a time the student will be able to recognise each vowel solely by the muscular sensations associated with its formation : he will be able to say to himself, ' Now my tongue is in the position for (i),' ' Now I have changed (i) into (ih),' &c., while not uttering the slightest sound, confident that if voiced or whispered breath is allowed to pass through the mouth the required sound will be produced.

48. The first requisite for analysing the formation of the vowels is the power of lengthening and shortening them without altering them in any way. In English, North German, and many other languages, short and long vowels differ not only in quantity but also in quality. If we compare the nearest conventional shorts and longs in English, as in ' bit' and ' beat,' ' not' and ' naught,' we find that the short vowels are generally wide (i, $\mathfrak{d}$), the long narrow (i, ɔ), besides being generally diphthongic as well. Hence originally short vowels can be lengthened and yet kept quite distinct from the original longs; (bɪit), for instance, = 'bit,' is quite distinct from (biit) = 'beat.' In the broad London pronunciation this lengthening of originally short vowels is extremely common. These observations will perhaps help the student to acquire facility in lengthening such a word as bit' without passing into ' beat,' and ' dog' into (dɔig) without making it into (dɔig). The shortening of narrow vowels, such as (ii) and (ui), will be found more difficult, but careful attention to the Scotch pronunciation of 'sick' and ' book' as (sik) and (buk), instead of (sɪk) and (bʊk), will be of great assistance.

49. After acquiring a full command of the separate vowels, the student should begin to compare them with one another, and note their relations. He should, for instance, compare the narrow and wide vowel pairs, such as (i) and (*i*), (u) and (*u*), until he feels clearly the common difference underlying them all. Also the rounded and unrounded, such as (o) and (ɐ). But this relation is most clearly seen in the front vowels, such as (y) and (i), &c.

50. The tongue positions may be compared in various ways. It is very instructive to run through a whole series either horizontally or vertically, shifting the tongue with uniform speed from one extreme position to the other. Thus, starting from (*i*), if the jaw is lowered continuously, while the current of voice is maintained, an indefinite number of vowel-sounds is produced till a broad (æ) is reached; if the tongue is stopped half-way, we have (*e*). Similarly, if we start from (æ), and retract the tongue, we obtain first (æh), and then the broad Scotch and London (*a*). In moving from the mixed to the back position the point of the tongue must be allowed to drop, which it naturally does when the root is retracted. Conversely, in moving from the back to the mixed position, the tongue must not only be advanced in the mouth, but the tip must also be allowed to rise slightly from its former depression [a].

51. The student can now proceed to acquire unfamiliar vowels. The importance of his previous training will now be manifest. He has only to follow the analogies of the changes he has already made, to produce without difficulty many sounds that he perhaps never heard before in his life. Thus, suppose he has learnt to

---

[a] If the tongue is advanced from the back position while the tip is kept down, the ' outer back ' position is formed. Cp. under § 66.

form (y), and pass with ease from (i) to (y), he only has to round (*i*) in the same way, and he will produce (*y*). Again, if from a comparison of (ʋ) and (o) he has learnt the medium degree of rounding that belongs to a mid vowel, he only has to apply it to (e), and he will have (ə). Conversely, if he has learnt to unround (o) into (ʋ), he only has to apply the same process to (ɔ) and (u) to obtain (ɴ) and (v)ᵃ. Mixed vowels are best learnt by arresting the transition between the nearest back and front vowels. Thus, if the student wishes to acquire the Swedish (uh), he only has to pass from (u) to (y) backwards and forwards several times without intermission, and then to arrest his tongue half-way ᵇ.

52. Finally, the different processes may be used to check one another. Thus, if the student has learnt to form (*a*) from (a) by lowering the tongue, he can also unround (ɔ), and if both operations are performed correctly, they will yield precisely the same sound.

Acoustic Qualities of Vowels.

53. We have hitherto entirely ignored the acoustic effects of the vowels. This has been done designedly. The first and indispensable qualification of the phonetician is a thorough practical knowledge of the formation of the

---

ᵃ Mr. Bell directs the beginner to spread the lips with the finger and thumb in unrounding. I find, however, that this method, although it succeeds with front, quite fails with back vowels, as it does not remove the inner rounding.

ᵇ Mr. Bell advises to attempt to blend the back and front articulations by pronouncing them simultaneously. I do not find that this succeeds in practice, as the student generally fails in the attempt to blend the back and front positions.

vowels. Those who try to learn new sounds by ear alone, without any systematic training in the use of their vocal organs, generally succeed only partially. Even in those exceptional cases in which a naturally quick ear combined with favourable occasions for practice enables a linguist to acquire an accurate pronunciation of foreign languages by imitation alone, his knowledge is little better than that of a parrot, for he is unable to record the sounds he has learnt, or to teach them to others, and the results of his labours perish with him. In the case of those who have only an average ear, and still more of those who have a defective ear, organic training is indispensable. There can be no question that flexible organs well trained together with only an average ear, will yield better results than even an exceptionally good ear without organic training. Nor must it be forgotten that fineness of ear is not necessarily accompanied by flexibility of the vocal organs. Indeed, what is commonly called 'an ear for sounds,' that is, the power of imitating sounds, depends quite as much on organic flexibility as on fineness of ear.

54. The test of 'ear' by itself is the power of discriminating and recognising sounds. This is an indispensable qualification for those who wish to write down sounds by ear, and must be carefully cultivated. To recognise a sound with certainty under the various differences of quantity, force, environment, &c., is no easy task, and requires long practice. The student should accustom himself to repeat the different vowels in a loud voice, and should compare those that are most like, till he is able to distinguish them. He should also, if possible, hear them pronounced by voices of different register and

quality, the effects of which are often confusing, especially
when a man's voice is contrasted with a woman's or
child's.

55. It will soon be observed that vowels whose formation is distinct are often very similar in sound. This will
be better understood if we consider that a vowel is,
acoustically speaking, voice modified by a resonance
chamber, viz. the mouth (the influence of the pharynx
being for the present ignored). Every time we change
the position of the tongue we create in reality a new
resonance chamber, which moulds the voice into a
different vowel. Every vowel can have its pitch raised or
lowered by varying the length of the vocal chords, as
when the scale is sung on any one vowel. But each
vowel has besides an inherent pitch of its own, due to the
shape and size of the resonance chamber. Thus, if (i),
(a), and (u) are all sung to the same note, we hear how
much deeper the pitch of (u) is than that of (a), while (a)
is also much deeper than (i). The best way, however, of
hearing the natural pitch of the vowels is to whisper them,
for the pitch of the whisper itself being invariable, the
differences caused by the resonance are clearly heard.
The connection between the size and shape of the resonance chamber and the pitch is self-evident. (i) evidently
owes its high pitch to its being formed by a narrow
channel in the front of the mouth, while the pitch of (a)
is lowered by the greater size of its resonance chamber,
and that of (u) by the narrowing of the lip-aperture, both
(a) and (u) being formed in the back of the mouth. The
wide forms of the front and mixed vowels are lower in
pitch than the narrow ones, because of the greater width
of the mouth cavity, but in the case of back vowels the

wides are higher than the narrows [a]. Rounding naturally lowers the pitch.

56. The following is the order of the vowels in pitch, according to Mr. Bell, beginning with the lowest.

u, u; o, o; ɔ, ɔ $\left\{ \begin{array}{l} v, \ a; \ v, \ a; \ v, \ \Lambda; \ æh, \ æh; \ eh, \ eh; \ ih, \ ih \\ ɔh, ɔh; \ oh, oh; \ uh, uh; \ œ, \ œ; \ ə, \ ə; \ y, \ y \end{array} \right\}$ æ, æ; e, e; i, i.

57. It is evident from this table that the same pitch may be produced by distinct modifications of the same resonance chamber, which agrees with the remark already made, that vowels whose formation is distinct are often very similar in sound (§ 55). Thus, starting from (i), we can lower its pitch either by retraction of the tongue, giving (ih), or by rounding, which gives (y), and consequently (ih) and (y) have the same pitch, and are so alike in sound that those who hear (ih) for the first time generally imagine it to be a round vowel. Again, English people who hear (œ) for the first time generally imitate it by their own (æh), and German phoneticians still regard E. (æh) and (v) as 'obscure' varieties of (œ) and (ə). Hence also the English imitation of the French (oh) or (oh) in 'bonne' by the English (v) in 'bun.'

58. It is also important to observe that such pairs as (i) and (e), (u) and (o), are as near in sound as (i) and (i), (u) and (u), which differ only in narrowness and wideness. The explanation is precisely analogous to

---

[a] 'Because,' as Mr. Bell says, 'the greater retraction of the tongue enlarges the oral cavity.' Of course, on Mr. Bell's theory of the cause of narrowing being in the pharynx, there is no *necessary* retraction of the tongue. On my view, however, this retraction is due to the convexity of the tongue, which in the case of narrow front vowels practically raises, instead of retracting, the surface of the tongue.

that of the similarity of (ih) and (y), namely, that the pitch
of (i) can be deepened either by widening into (*i*) or
lowering to (e), the result being nearly the same in both
cases, as shown by the French imitation of English (*i*) by
(e). Hence we get the following pairs of vowels extremely like in sound, and consequently very liable to be
confounded :

$$(i) \text{ and } (e) ; \quad (e) \text{ and } (æ)$$
$$(y) \text{ and } (ə) ; \quad (ə) \text{ and } (œ)$$
$$(u) \text{ and } (o) ; \quad (o) \text{ and } (ɔ).$$

59. The mixed and round pairs already exemplified are
also very close :

$$(\text{ih}) \text{ and } (y) ; \quad (i\text{h}) \text{ and } (y)$$
$$(\text{eh}) \text{ and } (ə) ; \quad (e\text{h}) \text{ and } (ə)$$
$$(æ\text{h}) \text{ and } (œ); \quad (æ\text{h}) \text{ and } (œ).$$

60. It is interesting to observe that these pairs are
often confounded even in vernacular speech. It very
seldom happens that[a] three such sounds as (e), (*e*), and
(æ) are kept distinct in a language, the general rule being
that when the distinction of 'close' and 'open' *e* is made,
(e) is the close sound, while the open one is represented
by (*e*) or (æ) indifferently. This is the case in English,
and it is impossible to determine whether (*e*) or (æ) is the
commoner sound in such words as 'head,' 'then,' &c.

61. As regards the acoustic relations of mixed vowels
to their corresponding fronts and backs, it must be noted
that unrounded mixed vowels resemble more their corresponding fronts, rounded their back vowels, as is indicated
by the symbols. The rounded mixed vowels owe their

[a] As in Danish.

'back' quality to their retention of the inner rounding of the back rounded vowels.

EXTENDED LIST OF KEY-WORDS.

62. The following extended list of key-words arranged under each vowel will, it is hoped, be useful to students, especially those who have to learn the sounds without a master. The contractions are the same as those already used in the general table (§ 43), with the addition of Da. = Danish, Du. = Dutch, Sw. = Swedish, Icel. = Icelandic. Each wide vowel follows immediately after its narrow.

63. ᴠ (high-back-narrow). According to Mr. Bell this vowel occurs in the Gaelic laogh (ᴌᴠɪ). It also occurs in Armenian (as pronounced to me by Prof. Sievers), for example, in the definite article (vz). This vowel, which offers difficulties to those who are not familiar with it, is best obtained by unrounding (u), following the analogy of the change from (o) to (ɐ), and checking the result by raising (ɐ) to the high position.

64. ᴀ (high-back-wide). According to Bell in the Cockney pronunciation of long *o*, as in (nᴀ[oh])='no.' It seems also to occur sometimes in the (ai) diphthong, as in (ᴀɪ[ih]) = 'I,' more commonly (eh[ih]).

65. ɐ (mid-back-narrow). English 'up,' 'come,' &c. Often tends to widening, (ɐp) becoming almost (ap).

66. a (mid-back-wide). E 'father,' 'papa'; N. G. 'vater,' 'mann'; Sw. 'man.' This vowel is liable to considerable fluctuations. It may be lowered nearly to (*a*), as in Italian and Spanish, where it is difficult to decide between (a) and (*a*). It may also be advanced almost to the (eh) position, the point of the tongue being kept down, giving a sound which is very like (æ), into which it is easily converted by raising the 'inner' front of the tongue towards the palate. If the point of the tongue is raised, it passes into (eh). This (ˌa) is the regular Danish sound, as in *mand* (mˌax'n), *mane* (mˌaɪneh), the long sound being still more advanced than the short. It is also the sound of the long Dutch *a*, as in 'v*a*der,' 'm*aa*n.' The French *a* tends also towards (ˌa).

67. *ɒ* (low-back-narrow). Frequent Sc. and provincial English sound of the *u* in 'b*u*t,'ˏ 'c*u*t,' &c., as in Sc. 'c*o*me *u*p!' (kɒm ɒp). It is also a common sound of short *a* in M. and S. G., as in 'k*a*ffee-k*a*nne.' Short *a* in Du. often has this sound, as in *a*l, v*a*t. It may be heard long in the vulgar London pronunciation of 'part,' 'park,' as (pɒɪt, pɒɪk), which are distinct from (pɔɪk, pɔɪt).

68. *a* (low-back-wide). Sc. 'm*a*n,' 'h*a*t,' &c. Sw. long *a*, as in 'f*a*der,' 'f*a*ra.' Mr. Bell identifies the long *a* in Italian with (*a*).

69. ih (high-mixed-narrow). According to Mr. Bell in a common American pronunciation of 'earth' as (ih[*i*]th). Also in the North Welsh 'tag*u*,' 'h*u*n,' &c. According to Mr. Bell the Russian 'jery' is (ihn).

70. *i*h (high-mixed-wide). Frequent in the E. pronunciation of 'pr*e*tty,' 'j*u*st' (written 'jist') and a few other words. Mr. Bell distinguishes the first and second vowel in 'fishes' as (*i*) and (*i*h).

71. eh (mid-mixed-narrow). G. Du. Dan. &c. unaccented *e*, as in 'gab*e*,' 'gerett*e*t'; 'dad*e*lijk' (daɪdehlehk); 'man*e*,' 'bevar*e*'. It is uncertain whether the Fr. 'que,' &c. has this sound or (ə). The sound is quite un-English.

72. *e*h (mid-mixed-wide). The E. unaccented vowels

in 'bigg*er*,' 'fav*our*,' '*a*ttack,' &c. seem to resemble this
vowel, or rather to fluctuate between it and the low-mixed
(æh) and (æh), but it is best to regard them as simply
'voice-glides' (§ 200). (*e*h) may be heard in the Swedish
'*ej*,' but apparently in rather a forward form (ˏeh[*i*]), while
in the E. '*eye*,' it is rather (ˏeh[*i*h]) or sometimes perhaps
(ˏa[*i*h]). Mr. Bell assumes (a) as the first element, considering (*e*h) 'Cockney,' but (a[*i*h]) is certainly not the
ordinary educatèd pronunciation, although even (a[*i*h]̄)
may be heard from the vulgar.

73. æh (low-mixed-narrow). E. '*err*,' 'b*i*rd,' &c. The
Icelandic short *ö*, as in 'skömm,' seems sometimes to have
this sound.

74. æh (low-mixed-wide). Frequent Sc. '*err*,' 'b*i*rd.'
Cockney '*u*p,' according to Bell.

75. i (high-front-narrow). Long Teutonic *i*-sound, as
in G. 's*ieh*,' Du. 'b*i*er,' Dan. 'hv*i*le,' Sw. 'hv*i*la.' Fr. f*i*n*i*,
f*i*n*i*r. Short in Sc. in many words, such as 'sick,' 'g*i*ve,'
'bu*i*ld.' Short in many Dan. words, such as 'g*i*k,'
'hv*i*dt,' 'at sp*i*lde.' The long E. *i* is a 'consonantal
diphthong' (i ɿj)[a], and its narrowness is often relaxed
almost to wideness.

76. *i* (high-front-wide). Short in E. 'f*i*n,' 'b*i*t,' in
Dan. 'f*i*k,' 'at f*i*nde,' 'at sp*i*lle,' and in N. G. 'k*i*nd,'
'b*i*tten,' where M. and S. G. have (i). Long in Icel.
'v*i*ta,' 's*y*nir.' It must be noted that the E. (*i*) is slightly
lower than in the other languages, verging towards (*e*).
The unaccented vowel in 'pit*y*' seems to be decidedly (*e*¹).

77. ѳ (mid-front-narrow). F. 'été,' 'aim*er*.' G. 's*ee*.'
Sw. 's*e*,' 'st*e*n.' Short in Sw. 'v*e*cka,' 'sk*e*pp.' (e) is

---

[a] See § 209.

often raised towards (i), and this (e¹) is the regular
sound in Dan., so that 'se' often sounds to an E. ear like
E. 'see.' (e¹) is also common in Edinburgh Sc.[a] Short
(e¹) in Dan. 'dette,' 'hende,' 'fred.' The E. sound is
lower than that of the other languages, is always diphthongic, and generally very feebly narrowed, fluctuating
between (eɪ[ih]) and (eɪ[ih]).

78. e (mid-front-wide). Occ. E. 'head,' 'end' (§ 61),
N. G. 'ende,' Dan. 'sted.' Long in Dan. 'læse,' 'træ.'
Interchanges frequently with (æ) in many languages.
(e) raised half-way to (i) is heard in the Sc. 'fill,' 'pit,'
and Du. 'lid,' 'kind,' neither of these languages possess-
ing (i). Also in E. 'pity' (§ 77).

79. æ (low-front-narrow). Usual E. 'hair,' occ. 'head,'
'end.' Very marked in Sc. 'head,' 'tell,' and Du. 'ben,'
'elf,' in which the position is lower than for the E. (æ).
Fr. 'père,' 'faire.'

80. æ (low-front-wide). E. 'man,' 'hat.' Long in
dialectic Dutch (North Holland) 'vader,' &c. The Dan.
long (ˌai) seems also to pass into (æɪ) sometimes. (æɪ)
may also be heard in the Swabian S. G. pronunciation, as
in (kæɪs)='käse.'

81. u (high-back-narrow-round). Short in Sc. and
Du. 'book,' and 'boek,' both=(buk). Long in G. 'gut,'
Dan. 'ude,' Du. 'voer.' F. 'sou,' 'tout,' 'tour.' E. long
(u) tends to (uɪw).

82. u (high-back-wide-round). E. 'good,' 'full.' The
N. G. (u) in 'und,' 'lust,' is rather closer than the E.

83. o (mid-back-narrow-round). G. 'so,' 'sohn.' Short
in M. and S. G. 'oft,' 'stock.' F. 'chaud,' 'peau.' The

----

[a] See Dr. J. A. H. Murray's 'Dialect of the Southern Counties of
Scotland,' p. 106 foll.

E. long (o) is diphthongal and of uncertain narrowness. It may also be noted that the G. (o) is more retracted than in F. and E., which gives it a deeper tone. For the Scandinavian (o) see § 42.

84. *o* (mid-back-wide-round). N. G. '*oft*,' '*stock*.' Occ. Sc. '*road*' (short). Long in Icel. '*hof*,' '*koma*' (often rather lowered towards ɔ), and in Welsh '*ton*.'

85. ɔ (low-back-narrow-round). E. '*law*,' '*lord*,' '*fall*.' Provincial long *a* in G. and Du. (perhaps also wide). For the Scandinavian (ɔ) see § 42.

86. *ɒ* (low-back-wide-round). E. '*not*,' '*dog*.' Often raised towards (*o*), producing various intermediate sounds. The short open *o* in Dan., Sw., and often in Icel. is (*o*) lowered towards (ɔ). Examples are Dan. '*folk*,' '*maatte*,' Sw. *folk*,' '*åtta*,' Icel. '*flokk*,' '*borg*.' These effects may, however, be due to various degrees of rounding, and the Scandinavian (ɒ) may be simply the wide form of the (ɔ) in '*maane*.'

87. uh (high-mixed-narrow-round). Swedish and Norwegian *u* in '*hus*,' '*ut*.' This vowel varies in character, according to the degree of retraction with which it is formed. In Sw. and Norwegian it often differs but slightly from (u). (uh) may often be heard in careless E. pronunciation, thus '*two*' is often (tuhɪw) or (t*u*hɪw).

88. *uh* (high-mixed-wide-round). Regular sound of the short *u* in Sw., as in '*upp*,' '*lund*,' '*rum*.' This latter word is nearly identical with an occasional E. pronunciation of '*room*.'

89. oh (mid-mixed-narrow-round). In what is called an 'affected' pronunciation of E. '*no*,' &c., the (o) is often advanced nearly to the (oh)-position.

90. *oh* (mid-mixed-wide-round). F. short *o* in '*homme*,' 'dotte.' May perhaps also be narrow. This sound may be obtained by pronouncing such words as 'follow' carelessly and rapidly (fɔl[ʌw]), and then prolonging the [ʌw] into (oh).

91. oh (low-mixed-narrow-round). According to Mr. Ellis this is the sound of the long *a* in Austrian G., as in 'euer gnɑden' (qɔhɪdn).

92. ɔh (low-mixed-wide-round). According to Mr. Bell this is the Cockney sound in 'ask,' &c.

93. y (high-front-narrow-round). F. 'lʉne,' 'aigʉ.' G. 'grün,' 'güte.' Du. 'zʉʉr.' Da. 'lys.' Short in Da. 'skyld,' 'at fylde,' and often in M. and S. G. 'schützen,' 'füllen.' There are various shades of difference to be observed in this vowel. The N. G. (y) is slightly retracted towards (uh). In Sw. and S. G. (y) is often imperfectly labialised, so that the (i) character is strongly marked.

94. y (high-front-wide-round). N. G. hʉtte. Dan. 'tynd,' 'bryst.' Icel. 'full,' 'lʉnd.' Long in Icel. 'hlʉt,' 'mʉna.'

95. ə (mid-front-narrow-round). F. 'peu,' 'vœu,' 'creʉse.' M. and S. G. 'schön.' Da. 'en ö,' 'at löse.' Short in S. G. 'götter,' 'stöcke,' and in Da. 'först,' 'at önske.' The Sc. sound in 'guɩd' seems to be (ˌə).

96. ə (mid-front-wide-round). F. jeʉdi, seʉlement (liable to interchange with (œ)). N. G. 'schön (ˌə), 'götter.' Da. 'en dör,' 'at göre.' Icel. 'ˌföt' (also pronounced (æhɪ), § 73).

97. œ (low-front-narrow-round). F. 'fleur,' 'beʉrre.' Sw. 'höra.' Short in Da. 'störst,' 'ström.' Interchanges constantly with (ə).

98. œ (low-front-wide-round). According to Mr. Bell in the Cockney pronunciation of 'out' (œɪt), 'hoʉse,' &c.

CONSONANTS.

99. A consonant is the result of audible friction, squeezing or stopping of the breath in some part of the mouth (or occasionally of the throat). The main distinction between vowels and consonants is that while in the former the mouth configuration merely modifies the vocalised breath, which is therefore an essential element of the vowels, in consonants the narrowing or stopping of the oral passage is the foundation of the sound, and the state of the glottis is something secondary. Consonants can therefore be breathed as well as voiced, the mouth configuration alone being enough to produce a distinct sound without the help of voice. Consonants can all be formed with whisper.

100. The friction of consonants may be varied by narrowing or widening the friction channel. The term 'hiss' implies audible friction of breath consonants, and 'buzz' of voice consonants.

Consonants admit of a twofold division (1) according to place, (2) to form.

101. *Place.* By place there are five main classes.

(1) **Back** (guttural) formed by the root of the tongue and the soft palate. Examples are (k) as in 'come,' (q) in 'si*ng*.'

(2) **Front** (palatal) formed by the front (middle) of the tongue and the roof of the mouth. (j) as in '*y*ou,' (n) as in F. 'Boulo*gn*e.'

(3) **Point**, formed by the point of the tongue and (generally) the upper gums or teeth. This class is

commonly called 'dental,' but the point of the tongue is not necessarily brought against the teeth. Examples of point consonants are (t), (n), (l).

(4) **Teeth.** Teeth consonants when formed by the point of the tongue may be considered as 'outer' (see below) varieties of point consonants. There is also a 'lip-teeth' consonant, (f). When outer point (or 'point-teeth') consonants are formed by placing the point of the tongue between the teeth they are called 'interdental.'

(5) **Lip.** S. G. *w* in '*w*ie,' '*w*o' is an example of a pure lip consonant. N. G. *w*=(v) is a 'lip-teeth' consonant.

Each of these positions admits of infinite subdivisions by shifting the tongue backwards and forwards, but it is amply sufficient to distinguish three varieties of each position, 'inner,' 'outer,' and 'medium,' the last being assumed as the normal position. The inner variety is denoted thus, (ₜt), the outer being (ₜt).

There are two special tongue modifications that require notice, 'inversion' (t↓) and 'protrusion' (t†). In inversion the point is turned back towards the soft palate, so that the narrowing or stopping is formed between the lower edge of the tongue-point and the top of the arch. In protrusion the tip of the tongue is extended to the lips. Inverted consonants allow of the distinctions of 'inner' and 'outer.'

Besides the simple positions there are 'mixed' or 'compound' consonants formed by narrowing, &c. the mouth channel in two or more places at once. Thus the E. (w) is formed not only by lip-narrowing, but also by raising the back of the tongue towards the soft palate; it is therefore a 'lip-back' consonant.

102. *Form.* By form there are also five classes:

(1). **Open** consonants are those in which the passage is simply narrowed without any contact, such as (kh) in G. 'ach' and Sc. 'loch,' (s), (th). The restriction as to contact applies only to the actual friction channel, and even then there may be slight contact, provided the current of breath is not impeded. Thus in forming (kh) the uvula often touches the back of the tongue, but without modifying the sound in any way, and even in (s) the tongue often comes into contact with the ridges of the gums without influencing the sound. In such a consonant as (f), on the other hand, the contact of the lips and teeth has the effect of forcing the breath to seek a channel elsewhere, namely through the interstices of the teeth, which form the real friction-channel. It is, however, also possible to form an (f) between the lips and the teeth without any contact.

(2). **Divided** consonants are formed by stopping the middle of the passage, leaving it open at the sides. The commonest type of this class is the 'point-divided' (l).

(3). **Stopped** (or shut) consonants are formed by complete closure of the mouth passage, as in (k), (d).

(4). **Nasal** consonants are formed by complete closure of the mouth passage, the nose passage being left open. If we take any stop, such as (b), and allow the air to pass through the nose by lowering the soft palate, we obtain the corresponding nasal, in this case (m).

When an unstopped (open or divided) consonant is pronounced with the nose passage open, it is said to be 'nasalised,' which is denoted by (*n*). Thus (j*n*) is a nasalised (j).

(5). **Trills** are a special variety of unstopped con-

D

sonants. They result from the vibration of the flexible parts of the mouth, either against one another, as when the lips are trilled, or against some firm surface, as when the tip of the tongue trills against the gum in forming a trilled (r). Their common character is due to the rapid periodic interruption of the breath by the contact of the vibrating body with that against which it is trilled, its elasticity (or, in the case of the uvula, its weight) causing it to resume its former non-contact, to be again driven back.

Trills are, therefore, intermediate between open (and divided) and shut consonants.

Trilling is indicated by (*r*), thus (*rr*) is the trilled (r).

TABLE OF CONSONANTS.

103. The annexed table will give a general idea of the relations of the principal consonants and of their symbols. As regards the latter it will be observed that (h) is used as a general diacritic sometimes to denote open as opposed to shut consonants, sometimes to indicate devocalisation. The front consonants, with the exception of (j), are indicated by the capitals of the small letters which stand for the corresponding points. The back-divided is denoted by (ŋ).

THE CONSONANTS IN DETAIL.

104. We can now consider the consonants in detail, with full examples.

Open Consonants.

105. kh (back-open). The normal (kh), as in Sc. and G. 'loch,' is formed between the back of the tongue and the middle of the soft palate. In (͵kh) the narrowing is formed as low and as far back as possible. It occurs in several S. G. dialects, especially those of Switzerland. If (kh) is formed near the place where the hard palate begins, we have (k̟h), which is the sound of *ch* in Scotch after front vowels, as in the exclamation (fikh). It must be noted that all back consonants are liable to vary their position more or less according to the vowels they are associated with, front and mixed vowels tending to advance the tongue from the normal medium position. These variations however, although natural, are not essential. The inner (͵kh) especially, generally preserves its position unchanged before all vowels. It must be understood that these different varieties are not all formed by the same part of the back of the tongue. The inner and outer varieties are formed, as far as the tongue is concerned, partly by shifting it backwards and forwards, partly by narrowing the passage by those 'inner' or 'outer' parts of the back of the tongue which lie nearest to the corresponding parts of the palate. These remarks apply to the front consonants as well.

106. gh (back-open-voice). Frequent G. *g* in 'tage,' 'wagen,' &c., where it is distinctly buzzed. When the passage is widened so as to remove all buzzing, the sound of (gh) no longer suggests (kh) or (g), but rather a weak (r) round. It is often difficult to determine whether the N. G. *r* in 'fahren,' 'hier,' &c. is a weak (gh) or a 'glide-vowel' (§ 207). When (gh) is squeezed, the breath

GENERAL TABLE OF CONSONANTS.

VOICELESS.

	Throat.	Back.	Front.	Point.	Point-teeth.	Blade.	Blade-point.	Lip.	Lip-back.	Lip-teeth.
Open	н, ʀh	kh	jh	rh	th	s	sh	ph	wh	f
Divided	—	ᴚh	ʟh	lh	ḻh	(lh)	(ˌlh)	(ph)	(wh)	—
Shut	—	k	ᴛ	t	ṯ	(t)	(ˌṯ)	p	(p)	(p)
Nasal	—	qh	ɴh	nh	ṉh	(nh)	(ˌṉh)	mh	(mh)	(mh)

VOICED.

	Throat.	Back.	Front.	Point.	Point-teeth.	Blade.	Blade-point.	Lip.	Lip-back.	Lip-teeth.
Open	ʀ	gh	j	r	dh	z	zh	bh	w	v
Divided	—	ᴚ	ʟ	l	ḻ	(l)	(ˌl)	(bh)	(w)	—
Shut	x	g	ᴅ	d	ḏ	(d)	(ˌḏ)	b	(b)	(b)
Nasal	—	q	ɴ	n	ṉ	(n)	(ˌṉ)	m	(m)	(m)

N.B. Letters enclosed in parentheses denote varieties for which no special signs are provided.

impulse being diminished enough to prevent any buzzing, an effect extremely like (g) is produced, as in the Icel. ' saga,' ' vega.'

107. jh (front-open). The front consonants admit of an inner and outer variety. (ˌjh) is formed on the hard palate near where the soft palate begins, the outer (jh) in the hollow of the arch. (ˌjh) and (ḵh) are, therefore, formed nearly in the same place. The essential difference is that the former is formed by the front, the latter by the back of the tongue. (jh) is often heard in E. in such words as 'hue,' and is the regular sound of Icel. *hj* in 'hjarta,' 'hjá.' The G. *ch* in 'ich,' 'nicht,' 'recht,' seems to vary between the medium (jh) and (ˌjh). The Norw. *k* before front vowels is pronounced (jh), as in 'kenna.'

108. j (front-open-voice). E. '*y*ou,' G. Du. Da. &c. *j* in 'ja.'

This consonant is often, as in E., and M. and S. G.[a], weakened into a vowel. (j) in N. G. is often distinctly buzzed.

Buzzed (ˌj) is the ordinary G. *g* in 'liegen,' 'regen.'

109. rh, r (point-open). The characteristic feature of (r) is that the friction passage is formed as much as possible by the tip alone. Hence the tip generally points upwards, and there is a tendency to make the outer front of the tongue concave, so as to prevent any front modification. The tongue being thus shortened, there is also a tendency to form the consonant further back than is the case with the other point consonants. The medium position for (r) is just outside the arch, and it cannot be formed at all in the interdental position. The outer (ˌr) is formed on the teeth-rim, the inner (ˌr) within the palatal

---

[a] See § 208, 3.

arch. E. *r* in 'red,' 'rearing,' is generally medium (r),
sometimes (ɹ). It is generally a weak, almost vocalic
squeeze, but after (t) as in ' try,' and, to a less degree,
after (d) as in ' dry,' it is distinctly buzzed [a].

In the western counties of England, and in Kent, the
inverted (rʇ) is the regular sound. The point is turned
back to where the fronts are formed, and the voiced
breath is squeezed between the palate and the lower side
of the inverted tip.

It must be noticed that buzzed and squeezed (r) have
very different acoustic associations, buzzed (r) is felt to
be allied to the sibilants, especially (sh) [b], while squeezed
(r) is felt to be a weakened form of (rr).

110. th (point-teeth-open). (th) is, like (r), formed by
the point. The essential difference between them lies in
the dentality of (th), which involves a more horizontal
position of the tongue, which has to be stretched out to
reach the teeth. In (r) the breath is checked by the
upturned point, in (th) there is secondary friction along
the extended front of the tongue.

There are several varieties. The most distinct is
formed by pressing the tip of the tongue against the back
of the teeth, and allowing the breath to hiss through the
interstices of the teeth. There is also an inner (ˌth), in
which there is no direct contact with the teeth, the tip
being merely approximated to the gum just behind the
teeth-rim. Outer (th) would be formed by putting the

---

[a] This was first noticed by Sievers (L. Ph. p. 52), who attributes
the abnormal narrowing of the (r) to the preceding stops, the tongue
not having time enough to withdraw itself from the palate to prevent buzzing.

[b] Sievers notices, in the passage just referred to, that E. ' tried ' can
hardly be distinguished from ' chide' by an unaccustomed ear.

tip between the teeth. Foreigners generally learn the (th) in this way, but it is doubtful whether this variety ever occurs in E. pronunciation. The medium (th) first described is often weakened by non-contact of the tip with the teeth, the contact being generally slight, and when the channel is much widened the hiss is almost lost, so that 'I think' sounds almost like 'I hink.' The essential feature of all varieties of (th) is that the breath is directed on to the teeth with the tip of the tongue.

(th) occurs in E., as in 'think,' 'faith,' 'author'; in Icel., as in 'þing,' 'þola'; and is the sound of the modern Greek θ.

111. dh (point-teeth-open-voice). In E., as in 'then,' 'with,' 'other'; Icel. ð, as in 'við,' 'það,' 'líða'; Modern Greek δ, as in δέδωκα (dhedhɔka).

112. s (blade-open). Like (th) this consonant owes its sibilance to the breath being directed on to the teeth, not however by the tip itself, but by the 'blade' of the tongue. This part of the tongue may be regarded as very forward front, hence Mr. Bell's definition of (s) as the 'front-point' consonant; but this name is ambiguous, as it is quite possible to pronounce the front (jh) and the point (rh) or (th) simultaneously, and the result is quite distinct from (s). The normal position for (s) is on the gums a little further back than for (th), the tongue being somewhat shortened. (͵s) is formed on the arch-rim, and is not uncommon in E., (ṣ) on the teeth. (ṣ) is the Spanish *c* and *z*, as in 'parecer,' 'razon.'

113. z (blade-open-voice). E. 'zeal,' F. 'zèle,' N. G. 'wesen.' (ẓ) is the Spanish soft *d* in 'ciudad' (ṣiuẓ·aaẓ).

114. sh (blade-point-open) is very similar to (s), but has more of the point element, which is the result of its

approximation not to (th) but to (rh)—(sh) is, in fact, (s)
arrested on its way to (rh). This is done by retracting
the tongue somewhat from the (s) position, and pointing
it more upwards, which brings the tip more into play.
Hence Mr. Bell's designation of ' point-front,' the prece-
dence of point implying predominance of the point
element. The name is ambiguous for reasons analogous
to those stated under (s).

The normal position for (sh) is naturally between that
of (s) and (rh)—near the arch. (ˌsh) is formed inside the
arch, (ṣh) near the teeth-rim. (sh), like (rh), cannot be
formed on the teeth, and being further removed from
them than (s) has less of the sibilant character, and consequently bears a close resemblance both to (rh) and
(jh).

(sh) occurs in E., as in ' she,' ' fish '; in F., as in ' chat,'
' cacher '; and in G., where it is generally labialised, in
' schön,' ' fisch.' Outer (sh) occurs in E. in the combination (tsh), as in ' church,' medium (t) being formed nearly
as much forward as (ṣh). The French (sh) seems to be
more forward than the E.

115. zh (blade-point-open-voice). E. ' rouge,' ' pleasure '; F. ' *juge*,' where it is more forward. (ẓh) in E.
(dẓh), as in ' judge ' [a].

[a] It will be seen that the above account of the mechanism of (s)
and (sh) agrees essentially with Mr. Bell's. Mr. Bell's son however has transposed the Visible Speech symbols for (s) and (sh), and
other phoneticians seem inclined to agree with him, chiefly, it appears, on the ground of the frequent development of (sh) in language
out of (s) followed by (j). But I think any one who will take the
trouble to pronounce (s) and (sh) before a looking-glass, throwing
a light at the same time into the mouth, will not fail to see that
the point of the tongue is clearly directed upwards in the change
from (s) to (sh). Theories of the historical development of sounds

116. ph (lip-open) is the sound produced by blowing to cool anything, or, in a stronger form, to blow out a candle. It appears to be an occasional sound of modern Greek φ. It is also a Japanese sound (§ 197).

117. bh (lip-open-voice). The M. and S. G. *w* in ' wie,' ' wo,' ' wein.' Spanish *b* in ' saber.' A troublesome sound for Englishmen, who confuse it with (w) on the one hand and with (v) on the other. It is best got by blowing to cool, and then vocalising, taking care not to raise the back of the tongue or narrow the cheeks, both of which together convert it into the E. (w).

118. f (lip-teeth-open). E. ' fife,' F. ' fief,' &c. This consonant may be formed with a strong hiss, by pressing the lower lip firmly against the upper teeth, and thus driving the breath between the teeth, or may be weakened by relaxing the pressure, or removing the lip entirely from the teeth, so that the friction channel is formed between the teeth-edge and the lip. When the hiss is much weakened (f) is very like (ph) in sound.

(f) is also very like (th), both agreeing in directing the breath on to the teeth, (th) by the tip of the tongue, (f) by the edge of the lip.

119. v (lip-teeth-open-voice). E. ' vie,' F. ' vie,' &c. The N. G. *w* in ' wie,' ' wo,' &c., is weaker than the E. and F. (v), being generally formed with very little buzz, so that it often strongly resembles (bh).

120. *Mixed Open Consonants.* All the open consonants are liable to be modified by some back, front, or lip

cannot be allowed to override facts that can be demonstrated by observation, and the change of (s) into (sh) under the influence of (j) may be easily explained as the result of simple retraction of the (s) towards the (j) position.

position. The most general in its effects is lip modification; for lip action, being independent of the movements of the tongue, can be applied to any tongue consonant whatever. Back and front modifications are, to some extent, dependent on the position with which the other element is formed, the pure point consonants, which leave the back and front of the tongue free, being most susceptible of them. The following are some of the more important mixed open consonants, arranged according to their leading (the first) element.

121. khw (back-lip-open). (kh) naturally passes into (khw) after (u), as in G. 'auch,' Sc. 'sough.' Initial (wh) also becomes (khw) by giving greater prominence to the back element in some Sc. dialectic pronunciations, as in (khwe¹lk)='which,' often written 'quhilk' [a].

122. ghw (back-lip-open-voice). Frequent G. *g* after *u*, as in 'zuge.'

123. jhw (front-lip-open). In G. (jh) after rounded vowels, as in 'züchtig.'

124. shw (blade-point-lip-open). This is the usual sound of G. *sch*, as in 'schiff,' 'fisch.'

125. wh=phkh (lip-back-open) differs from (khw) in the preponderance of the lip over the back action. E. 'which,' 'what'; Icel. 'hvít,' 'hvað.'

126. w (lip-back-open-voice). The E. (w) in 'we,' 'witch,' is always wide; it is simply (*u*) consonantised by narrowing the lip passage. Fr. *ou* in 'oui,' 'roi' (rwa), is consonantised (u). (w), being thus formed from back rounded vowels, preserves the inner rounding of those vowels, which is essential to its character. The true

---

[a] See Murray, Dialect of the Southern Counties of Scotland, p. 118.

' lip-back-open-voice' consonant is formed by retracting the back of the tongue while pronouncing (bh), and the result is quite distinct from (w), which requires cheek-compression as well, raising the back of the tongue to the full (u) position not being essential. (w) might therefore more correctly be described as the ' high-back-round-squeezed.' One result of this cheek-compression is that the lips are projected out instead of lying flat as in (bh), and this was formerly considered to be the cause of the difference between (bh) and (w). These remarks apply to (wh) also, although there the cheek-rounding is less essential.

127. bhj (lip-front-open-voice). Formed by pronouncing (bh), at the same time raising the front of the tongue towards the (j) position, or simply by narrowing the lip-opening of the vowel (y). This consonant is the F. *u* in ' lui,' ' puis.'

128. dhj (point-teeth-front-open-voice). Palatalisation is most easily effected with the inner variety of (th) and (dh), in whose formation the tongue is less stretched out. This (͵dhj), formed without any contact, is the Danish soft *d*, in ' gade,' ' gud,' ' vide.' When pronounced with a stronger hiss, as in the Jutland pronunciation, it has very much the effect of a palatalised (z). It is, however, pronounced very softly in Copenhagen. The palatal quality of the Danish soft *d* is clearly shown by the fact that such a word as ' bröd' (bʀəɪxˈdhj) sounds to an E. ear almost like (bʀəidh) [a].

129. sj, shj. These consonants appear to be common in the Slavonic languages.

[a] This (dhj) seems conclusively to disprove Mr. Bell's view of the E. (th) being a front consonant.

Divided Consonants.

130. ꞁh, ꞁ (back-divided). This, to unaccustomed organs, is one of the most difficult articulations. The centre stoppage is formed by the whole root of the tongue (which must be well pushed back), the breath escaping between the sides of the root and the back cheeks. (ꞁh) has not yet been found in any language; Mr. Bell compares its sound to the 'hiss of a waterfowl.' (ꞁ) is, according to Mr. Bell, the Gaelic *l* in 'laogh' (ꞁvɪ). It does not appear to be the Slavonic barred *l*, which is simply a variety of (l). Mr. Bell says that (l+gh) is often substituted for (ꞁ).

131. ʟh, ʟ (front-divided). An (l) or (lh) formed in the place of (j). A difficult articulation for those unfamiliar with it. The point of the tongue should in the first attempts be held firmly against the *lower* gums, so that the front may articulate by itself. (ʟ) is the Italian *gl* in 'gli,' Spanish *ll* in 'llano'[a]. The M. G. 'dorsal' *l* is a very forward (ʟ). According to Mr. Bell (ʟh) is a variety of defective (s) in E., formed apparently by the outer front of the tongue and the arch-rim.

132. lh, l (point-divided). The centre stop is formed by the flattened tip of the tongue against the gums just behind the teeth. It has the same inner and outer varieties as the other point consonants. There is also an inverted (l), which appears to occur in the eastern dialects of Norway, as in the name 'Ole'[b].

[a] In both languages with a (j) or glide-(i) following.

[b] I heard this very peculiar sound from Professor Storm of Christiania, but was unable to imitate it with certainty, and consequently cannot give any analysis of its formation. It sounded to

The back and front of the tongue being free in the formation of (l), it is capable of indefinite modification by alterations in the shape of the mouth, both by the movements of the tongue and by cheek and lip narrowing. The barred Slavonic (l) and the Dutch (l) in 'elf,' 'twaalf,' 'volk,' have a deep guttural character, due to concavity of the front and retraction of the back of the tongue. The same (l) may often be heard in the Sc. pronunciation of 'tell,' 'twelve.' In the F. 'elle,' 'aller,' and, generally speaking, in the Continental (l) the front of the tongue is raised towards the palate, which raises the pitch of the (l) and gives it something of the character of (ʟ). The E. (l) is formed without palatal modification, but without gutturality; it is, therefore, intermediate to the two extremes described[a].

(l) is generally formed without audible friction, but may easily be buzzed by spreading out the side edges of the tongue.

(lh) is the Welsh *ll* in 'llan,' the Icel. *hl* in 'hlaða,' *lt* in 'bilt,' and the French final *l* after consonants, as in 'table.' In all these cases it is the 'high' (half-palatal) (l).

133. There is also a 'lip-divided' consonant, formed by spreading out the lips and allowing the breath or voice to escape at the corners, keeping the lips firmly closed in the middle. This sound has not been found in any language.

134. There are also 'unilateral' varieties of the divided

---

me more like (r+) than (l+). It may have been a sound like the Japanese ([d]r), only inverted. (§ 243.)

[a] The above observtaions were made by me independently many years ago. I was, therefore, very glad to find them confirmed by Sievers (L. Ph. p. 55 foll.).

consonants, in which the breath or voice escapes on one
side only. The Welsh (lh) is often formed in this way
by allowing the breath to escape on the right side only.
They are indicated by (§) after the letter[a].

Nasal Consonants.

135. ꞯh, ꞯ (back-nasal). (ꞯ) in E. 'sing,' G. 'singen.'
Swedish 'sjunga,' 'regn.' This sound does not occur
in French.

136. N̲h, N (front-nasal). (N) is the F. *gn* in 'Boulogne,'
'vigne,' the Italian *gn* in 'ogni,' and the Spanish *ñ* in
'niño,' 'señor.' Like (ʟ) it is followed by (j) in all these
instances. Very forward (N) is the M. G. dorsal *n.*

137. nh, n (point-nasal). The E. (n) in 'nine' is the
medium one, formed on the gums a little behind the
teeth. The F. sound in 'nonne' is dental (͵n), often
interdental. In most of the Teutonic languages (n) is
generally dental, often also half-dental, part of the tongue
being on the gums, part on the teeth. (͵n), formed on
the rim of the arch, is not uncommon in English. (n͵)
is the 'cerebral' *n* of the Indian languages. It is distinct
from (͵n).

(nh) is the Icel. *hn* and *kn*, as in 'hníga,' 'hnut,' 'kníf.'

138. mh, m (lip-nasal). No examples are required of
this sound, the easiest of all consonants. (mh) may be
heard in that inarticulate substitute for 'yes,' which is
particularly frequent in Scotch (mmhm).

---

[a] There are also varieties of undivided open consonants, such as
(sh), formed on one side of the tongue. Sievers (L. Ph. p. 72) says
he has heard this (sh §) in English pronunciation.

Nasalised Consonants.

139. j*n* (front-nasal-open-voice) often occurs in careless French pronunciation as a substitute for (N).

140. Other nasalised consonants may be formed at pleasure, such as (r*n*), (s*n*), but the nasalised consonants are little used in language, on account of the great expenditure of breath they involve.

Shut (stopped) Consonants.

141. k (back-shut) admits of the same inner and outer varieties as (kh). (k) is the Arabic *kaf.*

142. g (back-shut-voice). This consonant does not exist in Dutch, except as a secondary modification of (k), when followed by a voice stop, as in ' bakboord,' ' zak-doek' (ba*g*boor*r*t, za*g*duk).

143. ᴛ (front-stop). A stop formed in the same place as (j). This is still the sound of the Sanskrit *ch,* as first accurately described by Mr. Ellis (E. E. P. p. 1120). The soft *k* in Swedish, as in ' kenna,' is often (ᴛjh).

144. ᴅ (front-stop-voice). This is the Sanskrit *j,* as still pronounced. It may sometimes be heard in the Swedish soft *g,* as in ' göra,' which is generally simple (j). The *gy* in ' Magyar ' seems to be (ᴅ).

Very advanced (ˌᴛ) and (ˌᴅ) appear to be the M. G. dorsal consonants.

145. t (point-stop). The E. (t) and (d) are formed in the medium position, but are often also (ˌt) and (ˌd). French (t) and (d) are dental, often also interdental. In most of the Teutonic languages they are either dental or half-dental, as with (l). Inverted (t) and (d) occur in some of the Indian languages, particularly in the Dravidian languages of the south, but are often confused with (͵t) and (͵d), as in the present North Indian pronunciation of Sanskrit (Ellis, E. E. P. p. 1096).

146. It is important to observe that E. (ᶜl) and (d), as well as (l) and (n), are often, especially in the medium position, practically 'blade-stops,' that is, the stop is formed not merely by the point of the tongue, but by the upper edge of the point and part of the upper surface inside the point, so that these 'blade' (t)s and (d)s are practically stopped (s)s. The common Continental half-dental (t) is also a blade consonant rather advanced.

147. d (point-stop-voice). The remarks made under (t) apply equally to (d). Interdental (d̟) occurs in the Cumberland dialect of E., as a substitute for (dh), as in 'father.'

148. p, b (lip-stop). These consonants require no remark.

It is also possible to produce a 'lip-teeth' stop, by covering the front of the upper teeth by the lower lip. The *p* in the G. *pf*, as in 'pfund,' is often formed in this way[a]. The corresponding voice consonant has a very soft effect, and closely resembles (bh). According to Prof. Land[b] the Dutch *w*, which is generally (bh), is also formed in this way.

149. *Mixed Stops.* Both back and point stops may be modified by simultaneous front contact.

kj (back-front-stop). This is the old-fashioned London *k* in 'sky,' 'kind,' with which the Icel. *k* in 'kæti,' 'kenna,'

---

[a] I was glad to find this observation of mine confirmed by Sievers (L. Ph. p. 68).

[b] Uitspraak en Spelling, p. 30. Cp. also Ellis, E. E. P. p. 1102.

is identical. (kj) always seems to generate a slight (j) or glide-(i) after it, like the simple front stops.

150. gj (back-front-stop-voice). Old-fashioned London sound of (g) in ' guide,' Icel. *g* in ' geta,' ' gæti,' with the same after-sound of (j).

151. In a similar way may be formed (tj) and (dj), and also (lj) and (nj), but the result is liable to be confounded with the simple (T), (D), &c. [a]

Trilled Consonants.

152. khr (back-trill). The uvula lies loosely on the tongue pointing towards the mouth. It is driven up by the outgoing air, and falls again by its own weight [b]. This is a common sound of *ch* in Swiss German and other S. G. dialects.

153. ghr (back-trill-voice). Northumbrian ' burr.' French ' *r* grasseyé.' A common substitute for (rr) both in whole districts, as in the M. G. Saxony, and individually.

154. rhr (point-trill). Welsh *rh*, Icel. *hr* in ' hríngr,' ' hross.' F. *r* final after consonants, as in ' théatre.'

155. rr (point-trill-voice). (rr) is much commoner than untrilled (r). It is the regular Scotch, Irish, French, Dutch, and Swedish sound. It is formed by bringing the tip of the tongue loosely against the gums, and directing a stream of voiced breath on it at the same time. The

[a] As was done by Mr. Ellis till the real meaning of Mr. Bell's front consonants was explained to him by Mr. Nicol (E. E. P. p. 1119). Mr. Bell, on the other hand, seems not to be aware of (kj) &c., for he makes the (kj) in ' kind ' to be simply an outer (k), from which it is certainly distinct.

[b] The best description and drawing of this consonant is that given by Merkel in his Physiologie der Sprache, p. 219.

fore part of the tongue must not be stiffened, or the trill is impossible.

156. phr, bhr (lip-trill).   The lips must be kept quite relaxed and protruded.   This consonant does not occur in any known language.

157. All of these sounds may be modified in various ways.   (rrj̈) occurs in Armenian, as pronounced to me by Prof. Sievers.

There is also a divided trill :—

158. Thr, Tr (back-divided-trill).   This difficult articulation has not been detected in any language.

159. Mr. Bell also states that (l) is capable of being trilled[a].

Glottal Consonants.

160. All of these are treated under other headings. For (H), the aspirate, see § 195 ; for (R) and (x) §§ 18 and 20.

Acoustic Qualities of Consonants.

161. The consonants are much easier to recognise by ear than the vowels, as far as their organic formation is concerned, and it is not till we come to synthetic distinctions of voice, &c., that their appreciation offers any particular difficulty.   The main practical difficulty with the consonants themselves is to form them with ease and certainty, many of them offering considerable difficulties to those unaccustomed to them.   The trills especially require long practice.

---

[a] It was formerly assumed that (r) and (l) were always *necessarily* trilled—on what grounds it is difficult to imagine.

162. The following table shows the pitch of the chief open consonants, according to Bell[a] :—

wh khw ʀh ‚kh kh f $\left\{ \begin{matrix} \text{ph} \\ \text{‚kh} \end{matrix} \right\}$ rh sh s jh th jh ‚jh

RELATIONS OF CONSONANTS TO VOWELS.

163. The main distinction between consonants and vowels is, as already indicated (§ 99), that consonants are independent of voice, vowels not. All breath articulations are therefore *ipso facto* consonants. Voice articulations are easily tested by opening the glottis: if they yield a distinctly audible friction, they are consonants. The buzz caused by the friction is often audible without devocalisation, as in the case of (z) and (dh).

164. If an open vowel, such as (a) or (æh), is submitted to this test, we obtain nothing but a sigh, which is inaudible except when pronounced forcibly. But if we take a high vowel, such as (i), and devocalise it, we obtain a hiss which is quite distinct enough to stand for a weak (jh). The same may be said of devocalised (u)= weak (wh). This would justify us in regarding (i) and (u) themselves as weak (j) and (w). In fact the boundary between vowel and consonant, like that between the different kingdoms of nature, cannot be drawn with absolute definiteness, and there are sounds which may belong to either.

165. In Scotch (iɪ) is often pronounced with a distinct buzz, and is then simply a held (j). In French also the (i) is often pronounced, if not with a buzz, at least

---

[a] (f) and (th) I have added myself. They are omitted by Bell, who regards them as divided consonants.

with a distinct consonantal squeeze, so that in such a word as 'guerrier' (gær je) it is difficult to know whether to call the *i* a vowel or a consonant. After a voiceless stop, where the (i) is devocalised, there can be no doubt as to its consonantal sound, as in 'pied' (p jhe). So also often finally, as in 'sympathie' (-t jhɪ). Similarly with (y) in 'vécu' (vek jhɯɪ).

166. On the other hand, there are many voice consonants which may be regarded as 'vowel-like' consonants. In fact, whenever a voice unshut consonant is pronounced without a distinct buzz, it is, to the ear at least, a vowel while being held. This applies especially to the voice nasals, which are, indeed, almost incapable of being buzzed (l) also, although it can be buzzed, is generally vocalic in sound. Lastly, (gh) and (r) can both be relaxed into sounds which are almost entirely free from friction, although they then may almost be regarded as vowels. But the friction comes out distinctly when any one of these vowel-like consonants is devocalised, and if they are consonants when breathed, they must be equally so when voiced. In the case of (l) and the nasals, although they have a purely vowel effect while being held, they always end with a distinct flap when the contact is broken, which unmistakeably proclaims their consonant character.

167. *Position.* The various positions of the open voiced consonants must necessarily yield more or less distinct vowel-sounds when expanded enough to remove all audible friction. The relations between the consonant and vowel positions are very important, and should be carefully studied. Thus, starting from the buzzed (gh), the student should carefully increase the distance between the back of the tongue and the soft palate till all friction ceases—he will thus obtain the vowel (a). If the movement is made very slowly, he will form the soft (r)-like (gh), producing a combination which suggests (gra).

168. The following are the more important of these relations[a] :—

ͺgh gh ˌgh ˌj j j ghᴡ ghᴡ ˌghᴡ,w ˌjw jᴡ ˌjᴡ
correspond to—

ᴅ ɐ v æ e i ɔ o   u   œ ə y

169. By weakening the different point and blade consonants a variety of vowels may be found, which are not included in the regular scheme of vowels.

170. If (r) is weakened we get a peculiar vowel-sound, which partakes of the character of (r) itself and of the mixed vowel (æh), the tip being raised while the rest of the tongue is nearly in the position for the low or mid mixed vowels. Most of the vowels may be modified by the tip in this way, and we thus obtain a class of point-modified vowels, represented by an (r) after the vowel-symbol. This (r)-vowel may be retracted, and we thus get another series of retracted-point vowels. In the Kentish pronunciation[b] the retracted (r) of 'sparrow,' &c., is thus incorporated into the preceding vowel, 'sparrow' being pronounced (spaɪrɹ↓).

171. By weakening (dh) a sound is produced which has quite the effect of a dental (r)-vowel. The Danish soft *d* is nearly this outer (r)-vowel, with the addition of front modification.

172. A weakened (z) gives a vowel which has the effect of a very forward (eh), being in fact the 'blade' vowel

---

[a] Based on Mr. Bell's tabulations, with additions of my own.

[b] As given me by Mr. Goodchild, of H. M. Geological Survey.

most nearly corresponding to (eh), and bearing the same relation to (eh) as (z) itself does to (j).

173. A weakened (zh) gives the point-modified blade vowel. It has the effect of a very forward (eh) with something of an (r)-quality. All these sounds may be combined, with various degrees of facility, with the other vowels. They may all be rounded.

174. If (bh) is weakened, with the tongue in the neutral (eh) position, we get (eh) with lip-rounding, which is about equivalent to inner (ə). If cheek-rounding is added, we have (oh)[a].

SOUNDS FORMED WITHOUT EXPIRATION.

175. All the sounds hitherto described imply expiration. It is however possible to form sounds both with inspiration, as is occasionally done in some Swiss dialects to disguise the voice[b], and without either expiration or inspiration, but solely with the help of the air in the mouth.

[a] The above remarks on the relations between vowels and consonants differ in some respects from those of Mr. Bell, who considers the mixed vowels (ih), (eh), and (æh) to be related to (z), (zh), and (r) respectively. It is true that if we lower the tongue from the weak (r) position, we ultimately get (æh), but the true (r) vowel is, as we have seen, something quite distinct from (æh), which is formed without any raising of the point. Again, if I consonantise (ih) and (eh), I get simply (j). (ih) may, of course, be made into a weak consonant simply by devocalisation, but the result bears no resemblance to (z), but is simply a slightly gutturalised (jh). It is in fact (ˌjh + jh), the mouth passage being narrowed in two places at once. If strengthened by raising the intermediate portion of the tongue, it passes entirely into (jh).

[b] See Winteler, ' Die Kerenzer Mundart,' p. 5.

176. 'Suction-stops' are formed in this way by placing the tongue or lips in the position for a stop, and then sucking out the air between the organs which form the stop; they are thus pressed strongly together by the pressure of the air in the mouth, so that when separated a distinct 'smack' is heard. These sounds are common in interjectional speech. Thus, if we denote suction by (ǂ) after the stop symbol, (pǂ) is an ordinary kiss, (tǂ) is the interjection of impatience commonly written 'tut!' &c. In many of the South African languages these suctions are those essential elements of speech known as 'clicks[a].' Thus in the Bushman language (pǂa) and similar combinations occur. In the Zulu language (tǂ) &c. are always accompanied by some other expiratory consonant. Thus (q) and (tǂ) are formed simultaneously, the (tǂ) not interrupting the (q)[b].

177. Other non-expiratory sounds are the implosives (§ 224), where, however, the following glide is, or may be, expiratory.

---

[a] This name is somewhat inappropriate: 'cluck' would describe the sounds better.

[b] See Bell, V. S. p. 125, for the Zulu clicks. Other clicks from American languages are described by Haldeman, quoted in Ellis, E. E. P. p. 1349.

PART III.

SYNTHESIS.

178. WE have hitherto considered sounds from a purely analytical point of view, that is, each sound has been considered by itself, as if it were a fixed, isolated element. But in language sounds are combined together to form sentences, and many sounds only occur in certain fixed combinations. Hence the necessity for synthesis as well as analysis. Analysis regards each sound as a fixed, stationary point, synthesis as a momentary point in a stream of incessant change. Synthesis looks mainly at the beginning and end of each sound, as the points where it is linked on to other sounds, while analysis concerns itself only with the middle of the fully developed sound[a].

Synthesis is either special or general, the former dealing with special combinations, the latter with sound-groups generally.

The most important general factors of synthesis, both special and general, are force, quantity, and the theory of 'glides,' or transitional sounds.

[a] Compare the remarks of Sievers, L. Ph. p. 75.

SPECIAL SYNTHESIS.

General Elements.

179. *Force.* Force, like quantity, belongs essentially to the synthesis of sounds, for it is always relative, always implying comparison, either of two different sounds or of different portions of the same sound, with which latter we are here concerned. Physically it is synonymous with the force with which the breath is expelled from the lungs, which is effected by upward pressure of the diaphragm. Every impulse of force is therefore attended by a distinct muscular sensation. Acoustically it produces the effect known as 'loudness,' which is dependent on the size of the vibration-waves which produce the sensation of sound. When we say therefore that one sound, or group of sounds, is uttered with more force than another, as in comparing the first with the second syllable of 'heavy,' we mean that in its utterance the air is expelled from the lungs with a greater muscular effort, that in consequence the size of the resulting sound-waves is greater, producing an effect of greater loudness on the ear.

180. It must, of course, be understood that force has nothing to do with pitch or tone (§ 270).

181. Force in its synthetic sense must also be carefully distinguished from those variations in the friction of unstopped consonants which are due to the varying width of the configurative passage. The friction of consonants is an essential element of their organic formation, and has no special connection with synthesis[a].

[a] There is, however, a certain connection between the audibility of the friction and the force of the outgoing air: a certain definite

182. We have now to consider the changes of force in a single breath-impulse, as for instance in pronouncing any vowel, such as (aɪ). Here we have three kinds of force, (1) level, (2) increasing (crescendo), and (3) diminishing (diminuendo), which may be symbolised thus—

level   a̿ɪ

increasing   a͛ɪ

diminishing   a͙ɪ

In examining the force of any stress-group it is a great help to whisper it, which gets rid of all disturbing tone-changes.

183. The general tendency of language is to pronounce with diminishing force. Thus in E the (k) of (kæt) is pronounced with more force than the (t). Hence also the end of a long is weaker than that of a short vowel, the force diminishing continuously throughout. Thus the (t) of ‘ cart ’ is weaker than that of ‘ cat.’ The same phenomena may be observed in German also[a]. In French, on the other hand, the force is more equal, the final (t) of ‘ tête,’ for instance, being pronounced with almost as much force as the initial one ; but even here there is no perfectly level force. < may be heard in interjections, as, for instance, in (aɪ) denoting joyful surprise. Here it is accompanied with a marked rise in pitch, but if whispered the < is unmistakeable.

184. The influence of force on the actual synthesis of language is extremely important. This subject will

position may produce audible friction under a strong impulse of breath, but not under a weak one. But the position itself is something absolute, and all articulation postulates a certain amount of force to be audible at all.

[a] See Sievers, L. Ph. p. 115 foll.

be fully discussed under General Synthesis. Here we
need only remark that the sense of unity and separation
is mainly due to force. As a general rule continuity
of force gives the impression of unity, discontinuity that
of separation. Thus (a͞i), (a͡i), and (a͞i), all have the
effect of single indivisible units, if prolonged ever so
much. But (a͡iĩ) and (a͞iĩ) sound like two distinct
units, even when there is not the slightest pause between
them.

185. *Quantity.* We may distinguish five degrees of
quantity or length :—

> very long
> long
> half long or medium
> short
> very short,

but for practical purposes the three distinctions of long,
half-long, and short are enough. Long is denoted by (ɪɪ),
half-long by (ɪ) after the sound symbol, and short is left
unmarked. If only two degrees are marked, (ɪ) is used
for long, short being unmarked.

186. The quantity of any one sound is apt to vary
according to its circumstances. Thus in E. final long
vowels, as in 'see,' and before voice consonants, as in
' seize,' are really long, while before breath consonants
they are shortened to half-longs, as in ' cease.' But in
German full length is preserved before voiceless consonants as well as voice ones, so that the (o) in 'noth' is
as long as the E. 'node,' not half-long as in ' note.'

In many Scotch dialects there are no full long vowels
at all, all long vowels being shortened to half-longs.

187. In some languages, such as F., the distinctions of

long and short are not clearly marked. In French most
vowels are half-long, and are only occasionally lengthened
or shortened into full longs and shorts. In French, distinctly short accented vowels are generally final, as in
' oui,' which is directly opposed to E. usage.

188. The distinctions of quantity apply to consonants
as well as vowels. Thus in E. final consonants are long
after short, short after long vowels, as in (hilı), (hiıl)=
' hill,' ' heel.' (l) and the nasals are long before voice,
short before voiceless consonants, as in (bilıd), (bilt)=
' build,' ' built.' Even stops are lengthened finally after
short vowels, as in (bædı)=' bad.' The E. student should
practise lengthening and shortening consonants under all
circumstances. The short final consonants after short
vowels will be found difficult. They may be heard in
German pronunciation, as in ' mann,' ' hat,' and still more
clearly in Danish, as in ' ven,' ' hat,' which have a very
abrupt sound to English ears.

189. *Glides* [a]. Synthesis introduces us to a special
class of elements called ' glides,' or transitional sounds,
produced during the transition from one sound to the other.
Thus, in pronouncing any combination, such as (ki),
we have not only the two sounds (k) and (i), but also the
sound produced in passing from one position to the other.
This ' glide ' differs from the two extremes (k) and (i) in
having no fixed configuration, it is, in fact, composed of
all the intermediate positions between (k) and (i), through
which it passes without dwelling on any of them. If the
tongue were arrested at any one intermediate point, a

---

[a] This term was first used by Mr. Ellis. Mr. Bell also adopted
it, but limited its application to glide-vowels. I use it here in the
same sense as Mr. Ellis.

single definite sound would be produced, and instead of
one uninterrupted glide from (k) to (i), we shall have two,
one from the (k) to the intermediate point, another from
there to the (i).

190. It would clearly be impossible to symbolise all the
infinitesimal intermediate positions of which a glide is
made up; nor is it ever necessary, the general principle
being that in all cases of transition from one fixed
position to another the shortest way is taken : given, therefore, the symbols of the fixed positions, the character
of the glide follows as a matter of course. Glides are
implied simply by the juxtaposition of the symbols of
the fixed positions between which they lie, as in the case
of (ki).

191. Besides these essential, implied glides, there is
another class of 'unessential' glides, which require to be
written separately. Thus, instead of passing direct from
(k) to (i), the organs can move up to the (u) position, and
without stopping there pass on to (i). Here there is a
continuous glide from (k) to (i), but it is a roundabout glide,
and not implied by the positions of the (k) and (i). These
'glide-sounds' (glide-vowel in the present case) have a
definite, though not a fixed configuration. Thus, in the
present case, there is an essential glide implied from the
(k) to the (u) position, and from there to the (i) position,
and the (u) position is therefore the distinct *limit* of the
glide-vowel, but it is itself no more a fixed configuration
than any one of the intermediate positions between it and
the (k) or (i) positions—like them it is simply one of a
series. These glide-sounds are symbolised by being
enclosed in brackets, thus (k[u]i), distinct from (kui), in
which the (u) position is maintained unchanged for an

appreciable period. The brackets are omitted whenever it can be done without causing ambiguity.

192. Glides are distinguished according as they precede or follow the sounds as 'on'- and 'off'-glides [a]. Thus the glide in (ki) is the off-glide of (k), the on-glide of (i). Initial glides, such as the on-glide of (k) in (ki), which are only preceded by a silence, are generally inaudible. Final, or 'on-silence' glides, such as the off-glide of (k) in (ik), are generally audible.

193. The acoustic effect of glides varies according to the force and the rapidity with which they are pronounced. If the transition from one position to another is made very rapidly and with slight force the glide is hardly heard at all, although any break, however slight, would at once be heard. On the other hand, even an essential glide, if formed slowly and with a certain force, is often heard as a separate element. Thus in such a combination as (aja) there is always an essential glide from the first (a) to the (j), but if the (a) is pronounced with rapidly diminishing force, and a second force-impulse follows on the (j), thus (ājā), the glide is not noticed at all; whereas, if the transition is made slowly and with only a gradual alteration of force, the glide from the (a) to the high-front position is distinctly heard, and the effect is (a[i]ja) [b].

194. The distinction between glide and fixed configuration is not so clearly marked in the consonants as in the vowels, and it is often doubtful whether a consonant is not to be considered rather a glide than a fixed element. This applies especially to initial consonants, such as (s)

---

[a] The names were first suggested by Mr. Ellis.

[b] What Mr. Ellis describes as *absence* of glide is rather *weakness* of glide.

and (l) in (sa) and (la), where the position is only momentary, and most of all to the aspirate (ʜ), which seems to vary indefinitely between glide and fixed configuration [a]. The breath stops are pure glides acoustically (§ 211). These fluctuations make it impossible to apply the sign [ ] with perfect uniformity.

VOWELS.

INITIAL AND FINAL VOWEL-GLIDES.

195. Vowels may be begun and finished in various ways [b].

(1) The glottis is gradually narrowed, passing through the various positions for breath and whisper till voice is produced. This gives the 'gradual' beginning ([ʜ]a), which is the ordinary way of beginning a vowel.

(2) The breath is kept back till the glottis is closed for voice, which begins at once without any introductory breath. This is the 'clear' beginning ([ʌ]a), well known to singers, who are always taught to avoid the 'breathy' gradual beginning.

In both these cases the stress, or force-impulse, of the syllable begins on the vowel. If the stress begins on the glides they are at once recognised as independent elements, [ʜ] giving (ʜ) [c], the ordinary 'aspirate,' or letter *h*, while [ʌ] develops into (x), the glottal catch, which is

---

[a] Cp. § 197.
[b] Cp. Ellis, E. E. P. p. 1129.
[c] Written simply (h) whenever it can be done without causing ambiguity.

practically a stopped consonant, just as (н) is an open consonant, or consonant-glide [a].

196. It is important to observe that mere 'breath' (the open glottis) is sometimes distinct from aspiration. The feeble friction of breath passing through the open glottis is heard equally in all the passages above the glottis, while that of (н) is distinctly localised in the narrowed glottis.

197. Although (н) is essentially a transition sound between breath and voice, it is not therefore necessarily a glide, and indeed it often happens that some definite narrowing of the glottis is held a moment before voice is formed [b]. (н) is, however, liable to have its character modified by the configuration of the mouth; and the position for the vowel which follows the (н) being generally assumed, or at least prepared, while the (н) is being formed, the (н) naturally assumes the character of that vowel. It is in fact the voiceless (or whispered) glide-vowel corresponding to the vowel it precedes [c], and it is easy to tell by the sound of the (н) what vowel is to follow [d]. (н) is therefore in the glottis a consonant, in

---

[a] The distinction between the gradual vowel-beginning and (н) is a very instructive instance of the importance of force in determining the synthesis of sounds. The mere force with which the breath is driven through the narrowed glottis is of secondary importance—the real distinction lies in where the force begins. In (на) we may pronounce the (н) with as much force as possible, but if a fresh impulse, however slight, begins on the (a), we hear simply (a) with the gradual beginning, whereas the gentlest stress, if it only begins on the (н), and is carried on to the (a) without discontinuity, gives the effect of (на).

[b] According to Czesmak this is usually the case.

[c] It may also precede consonants, such as (l) &c.

[d] This was noticed by Mr. Bell, who communicated it orally to me many years ago.

the mouth a voiceless glide-vowel [a]. (н) before (a) has a back, before (i) a front quality, and if exaggerated (нa) and (нi) develope into weak (kha) and (jhi). In Japanese the aspirate varies in this way before different vowels. Before high vowels it has a distinctly consonantal effect (jhiɪ, phʊhɪ), while before mid-vowels it seems to be merely a strong aspirate (нaɪ, нeɪ, нoɪ) [b].

198. Vowels are finished in different ways analogous to those in which they are begun.

(1) By a gradual opening of the glottis, the final glide passing through whisper to breath, which gives the 'gradual' ending.

(2) By a cessation of expiration while the glottis is still closed for voice, giving the 'clear' ending.

If uttered with stress, after the vowel (a) for example, (1) becomes (aн), which is still the Sanskrit visarga [c], and (2) becomes (ax), the Danish 'stödtone' (§ 19).

199. Final (н) has a consonantal character when pronounced forcibly, especially after the high vowels. If the high position is relaxed slowly the consonantal hiss becomes very marked, even if there is but little force on the

---

[a] Mr. Ellis regards the normal (н) as simply a 'jerk of the voice,' without any breath. Mr. Ellis's own pronunciation does not appear to me to differ essentially from my own. He simply reduces the breath effect to a minimum by contracting the glottis and giving a short impulse of force, passing on at once to the vowel, which, of course, gets rid of the 'breathiness' which so often accompanies the (н). Mr. Ellis's (нa) is in fact almost ('ʌa). The only 'jerk of the voice' I can produce is (xa).

[b] I find, on referring to my notes on the pronunciation of the same Japanese gentleman who dictated the sounds to Mr. Ellis, that I wrote (khaɪ), (khoɪ), and (нeɪ), the last only agreeing with Mr. Ellis's appreciation. This will show how difficult the distinction is.

[c] Ellis, E. E. P. p. 1139.

F

glide. The Icelandic final (i) and (u) are pronounced in this way, as in '1' and 'nú' (iᴎ, nuᴎ), almost=(iɪjh, nuɪwh). So also in Danish, often also in Dutch.

Glide-Vowels and Diphthongs.

200. Glide-vowels generally occur in combination with full vowels (vowels formed by a fixed configuration), forming 'diphthongs,' to which we will return immediately. Undiphthongic glide-vowels occur however also, the commonest of which is the 'voice-glide' [ʌ], produced by emitting voice during the passage to or from a consonant. It has no definite relation to any one vowel, although it approaches most nearly to the neutral vowel (eh) or (æh). The voice-glide is an essential element of many combinations, and often occurs as an unessential element in such words as 'against' ([ʌ]gænst), 'bigger' (b*i*g[ʌ]), 'together' (t[ʌ]gædh[ʌ]), &c. It may be rounded, and this [ʌ*w*] may be heard in a rapid pronunciation of such words as 'foll*ow*.'

A diphthong is the combination of a full vowel with a glide-vowel before or after it. Thus, if we place the vocal organs in the position for (i), and then allow voice to sound while passing from the (i) to the (a) position, and hold the (a) long enough to give it a fixed character, we have the diphthong ([i]a). If we begin with a full (a) and then pass to the (i) position, letting the voice cease as soon as the (i) position is reached, we have (a[i]).

201. These are the *essential* elements and conditions of every diphthong. The glide-vowels can, however, be held or lengthened into true vowels without destroying the diphthongic character of the whole combination, pro-

vided the continuity of stress be observed (§ 184). Thus
(a͡[i]iɪ ...) may be prolonged to any extent, and the whole
group will still be felt to be one diphthong.

202. In the Quantity of diphthongs we must distinguish
between the quantity of the vowel and of the glide, which,
if we allow only long and short quantity, gives four
varieties :—

(1) a[i]
(2) aɪ[i]
(3) a[iɪ]
(4) aɪ[iɪ]

(2) is heard in the E. ' say,' and (3) is the quantity of E.
' eye.' The lengthening of the glide in ' eye' is to com-
pensate for the shortness of the vowel : if both vowel
and glide were short, we should have a short monosyllable,
which is contrary to the general character of E. (§ 188).

In E. the older diphthongs of the (ai), (au), and (oi) type
have short vowels and long glides, while the later diphthongised (eɪ) and (oɪ) have the vowel long and the
glide short.

203. The length of diphthongs before consonants in E.
varies according to the consonant. Before voice consonants they have the same length as when final, as in
' rise,' ' ride '=(3), ' save,' ' raid '=(2), but before voiceless
consonants both vowel and glide are shortened, the final
consonant being lengthened by way of compensation, as
in 'rice,' 'write'; ' race,' ' rate.' If the diphthongs in these
words are isolated by suppressing the final consonants, it
will be found that they have an abrupt effect, quite different from that of final ' eye,' &c.

204. The popular conception of a diphthong is, to a

great extent, dependent on the associations of written
language. Diphthongs in which the glide precedes the
vowel, 'fore-glide diphthongs,' are generally denoted in
written language by a consonant, and hence the glide is
generally assumed to be a consonant, or else these diphthongs are called 'spurious,' it being supposed that the
connection between their elements is less intimate than in
the case of other diphthongs.

205. Of the diphthongs in which the glide follows the
vowel, 'after-glide diphthongs,' the most frequent are
varieties of what may be called the (ai) and (au) types, as
in 'high' and 'how.' It has accordingly been laid down
as a general law that in all diphthongs the movement must,
as in these diphthongs, be in the direction of narrowing,
and that 'none others are genuine.'

206. Again, it has been assumed from the spelling *ai*
and *au* that the second element of these typical diphthongs must necessarily be (i) and (u), whereas the fact is
that they usually stop at some lower position.

Until these prejudices are got rid of, no one can attempt
the very difficult task of analysing diphthongs into their
elements [a].

207. The peculiarity of diphthongs is that their elements may vary almost indefinitely, if only the *general
relations* of glide and vowel are preserved. The following
general laws may be laid down.

(1) Glides (that is, glide-vowels) before a vowel have
the effect of consonants.

(2) Back-glides before and after vowels have the effect
of (r). Examples:—[*a*]i, [u]æ, i[ɔ], e[*a*].

---

[a] Mr. Bell's 'glides' are, as Mr. Ellis has remarked, 'mere
evasions of the difficulty' (E. E. P. p. 1151).

(3) Front-glides before a vowel have the effect of [j]:—
[*i*]a, [i]æ, [æ]u.

(4) Glides after front vowels which have an upward movement, and glides after back vowels which have a forward and upward, or simply forward movement, have the effect of [i], as in (ai), e[i], œ[e], a[æ], a[eh].

(5) Round-glides which move upwards (not forwards as well) after back, or upwards and backwards after front vowels, have the effect of [u] as in (au), (if the movement is downwards the effect is that of (r*w*):—a[*o*], o[u], æ[u].

The glides may be rounded without disturbing these general relations.

Mixed-glides have a somewhat doubtful character. The high-mixed has quite a front character in diphthongs, whereas the low-mixed has more of the back quality, the mid-mixed being either front or back in its character according to the direction of movement.

208. A few actual examples may now be given of each category.

(2) [*u*] frequently occurs as a substitute for (r), as in ([*u*]æd)='red.' Before another (*u*), as in ([*u*]*u*k)= 'rook,' it is not very distinct, but is still distinctly audible. Here there is no change of position whatever, and the distinction between glide and vowel is simply one of force, the beginning of the ([*u*]*u*)=(*u*ɪ) being pronounced with weak stress, which suddenly becomes stronger, and is held a moment at its greatest degree. If the (*u*ɪ) is pronounced with gradually increasing force the vowel is heard simply as a long (*u*). It must, however, be understood that there is nothing in the sound of ([*u*]*u*k) that *necessarily* suggests a glide. It is only the frequent hearing [*u*] for (r) in such words as 'red,' where it is

distinctly audible, that prepares the ear to expect it in other familiar combinations.

[æh] or [æh], or the simple voice-glide [ʌ], is the regular E. substitute for (r) wherever the (r) is not followed by a vowel, as in 'here' (hɹɪ[æh]), 'there' (dhæɹ[æh]), 'ore' (ɔɹ[æh]). In 'affected' pronunciation there is a further retraction of the glide to the (*a*) position.

All these substitutes for (r) are closely allied to weak (gh), and it is not always easy to determine whether the sound is a consonant or a glide-vowel.

(3) The E. *y* is often weakened into glide-(*i*h), as in 'you,' 'young,' or perhaps also into raised (*e*). All the front-glides may have the effect of a (j) before other vowels, the effect being of course most marked when the glide is closer than the vowel. If fact ([æ]i) would hardly suggest (ji) at all, but rather (æ[i]), according to the next class.

(4) These diphthongs, as far us the unrounded ones are concerned, fall into two main groups, the (ai) and the (ei) type, according as the first element has a back or a front character. When the vowel is (e) or (*e*), there can, of course, be no doubt as to the character of the diphthong, any more than when the vowel is a back one. But when it is (æ) or (*æ*) the combination has almost the effect of a very forward diphthong of the (ai) type. Thus the first element of 'long *a*' in English, as in 'take,' is generally (e) or (*e*), but in the broad Cockney pronunciation it is (æ), and the resulting diphthong is not only heard as belonging to the (ai) type, but actually passes over to it, the first element becoming the mid-mixed (*e*h), as in the ordinary pronunciation of 'eye' [a].

[a] I believe, however, that those who thus broaden the diphthong

As already remarked, the second element of these diphthongs is not necessarily (i), but may be some lower vowel. Pure [i] or [*i*] may be heard in the Icelandic diphthongs, as in 'nei' (neiʜ), 'sæ' (saiʜ) [a], also in the common Dutch diphthongised *ee*, as in 'been' (beɪin). In E. the glide is always wide, and never seems to reach (*i*). Its precise nature is difficult to determine, but it seems to be generally (*i*h) [b].

Sievers makes out the glide in the German *ai* to be (e)[c], by which he may however mean [e¹]. The broad London (aɪ*i*h) frequently shortens the distance between glide and vowel by substituting the neutral (*e*h) for (*i*h), giving (aɪeh), which makes 'pie' sound like 'pa.' This (*e*h)-glide may also be heard in Scotch pronunciation.

If the vowel is a rounded one, we get various diphthongs of the (oi) and (əi) type, according as the vowel is a back or front one, such as the E. diphthong in 'boy' (boeh), and the Icel. *au*, as in 'launa' (ləina).

Rounding of the glide does not alter the character of these diphthongs. The G. *eu* in some of its varieties is an example, 'neu' being pronounced (naə) and (noə), in N.G. (no*i*) or rather (no[e¹]).

(5) These diphthongs are closely analogous to those

in 'take,' generally keep it distinct from that of 'eye,' by making the first element of the latter (a) or (*a*).

[a] I am not certain of the narrowness of the [i]; Mr. Ellis writes [*i*].

[b] I have sometimes thought it was raised (*e*); possibly both occur, as (e¹) might easily pass into (*i*h).

[c] L. Ph. p. 87. Sievers's ingenious proof, which consists in introducing two fingers into the mouth so as to form an artificial palate, can also be applied to English: it will be found that perfectly good (ai)-diphthongs can be formed under these circumstances, but no (i).

just described. Like them, they fall into two classes, the (ou) and the (au) type, according as the first element is regarded as a rounded or an unrounded vowel. Just as there is a broad (ai)-like form of (ei*i*h), so the regular (o*ıu*) varies as (o*ıu*) and (ɔ*ıu*), which last has very much the effect of (au), so that (nɔ*ıu*)='no,' seems really to pass into (nɑ*ıu*)[a]. It is, however, difficult to distinguish between (ɔ*ı*) with its rounding reduced to a minimum and (ɑ*ı*) pronounced, as it often is in English, with half-closed mouth.

The first element of the (au) type is often represented by a mixed vowel, as in the E. *how* (hæhoh).

It will be noticed that the glide-vowel of the (au) type is simply the neutral vowel rounded, just as that of the E. (oi)-diphthong is the unrounded (*e*h). The German *au* in 'haus,' has, according to Sievers, (o) for its glide—(haos) or (hɑos)[b]. In (o*ıu*) there is generally no change at all in the tongue position, the lips being, simply narrowed as for (*u*). The second element is then the wide form of the Scandinavian (o)[c]. There may, however, occasionally be also a slight raising of the tongue as well.

Of diphthongs of the (iu) type, whose first element is a front-vowel, there are no certain examples. The nearest approach is the American diphthong in 'new,' which Mr. Bell writes (n*iy*). These diphthongs, in which the glide is simply the vowel rounded, of which the G. (a*o*)= *au* is also an example, form, strictly speaking, a class by themselves.

---

[a] In the pronunciation of those who seem to make 'no' into 'now' the first element of 'ow' becomes distinctly (æ), so that the two diphthongs are kept perfectly distinct.

[b] Perhaps rather (hɑos)?　　　　　　　　　　[c] See § 43.

Consonantal Diphthongs.

209. The mid-vowels (eɪ) and (oɪ) are diphthongised by raising the tongue towards (i) and (u). If we attempt to diphthongise (iɪ) and (uɪ) in the same way, they necessarily develope into consonants (iɪj), (uɪw). If the consonants are simply squeezed, not buzzed, the combination has quite a diphthongic character, as in the usual E. pronunciation of 'he,' and 'who.' There are several intermediate stages possible. Thus, if the vowel position is slightly lowered, a diphthong may be produced simply by moving the tongue up to a closer, but still a vowel position. This seems to be often the case with the English (iɪ). In 'who' there can be no doubt as to the final consonant.

In E. the vowels themselves are generally half wide, half narrow, though they may also be quite wide.

CONSONANTS.

210. All consonants consist of three elements, (1) the consonant itself, (2) the on-glide, and (3) the off-glide. Each of these elements may be either voiceless or voiced, and may be modified in various other ways. Consonant synthesis is most clearly seen in the stops, whose synthesis is at the same time the most important.

Stops.

211. The great peculiarity of voiceless stops is that in themselves they have no sound whatever, they are, acoustically speaking, pure glide-sounds, which are only audible in the moment of transition from or to some other sound. Voice stops, on the other hand, can have a distinct sound of their own in addition to that of their glides, but as stops can only be voiced by driving voiced breath into an air-tight chamber[a], they cannot be continued for any length of time.

212. Confining our attention for the present to the off-glide, we may distinguish four chief kinds of voiceless and voice stops : (1) voiceless stop and breath glide (k[ʜ]a) ; (2) voiceless stop and voice glide (k[ʌ]a) ; (3) voice stop and breath glide (g[ʜ]a) ; and (4) voice stop and voice glide (g[ʌ]a). These sounds may be heard in initial (k), initial (g), final (g), and (g) between vowels respectively.

(1) In (k[ʜ]a), as in (ka-), the glottis is left open while the stop is being formed, and the chords are not brought into the voice position till the moment of loosening the stop, so that before the glottis has time to form voice there is a slight escape of breath between the stop and the vowel—the glide from the stop to the vowel is breathed.

(2) In (k[ʌ]a), as in (ga-), the glottis is in the position for voice during the stop, but without any air being forced through it, and consequently the stop is as inaudible as in the case of (k), but voice begins the moment the stop is loosened, and the glide is therefore voiced.

(3) In (g[ʜ]), as in (-ag), the voice runs on from the vowel to the stop without break, but the glottis is opened simultaneously with the loosening of the stop, which causes a puff of breath, just as in final (-ak).

(4) In (g[ʌ]), as in (aga), the voice runs on from vowel to vowel without intermission, both stop and on- and off-glide being voiced.

[a] Forming what German phoneticians call a ' Blählaut.'

213. Consonants with voiceless stop and breath off-glide are called 'breath' or 'voiceless' stops; consonants with voiced stop are called 'voiced' stops; and those with voiceless stop and voice glide (ga-) may be called 'half-voiced' stops.

214. It appears, then, that initial, medial and final (g) are really three distinct sounds. Initial (g) is (k[H]), medial (g[ʌ]), and final (g[H]). (k), on the other hand, is always the same—(k[H])[a].

215. The following table gives all the possible combinations, initial, medial, and final:—

INITIAL.	MEDIAL.	FINAL.
*k[H]a	*ak[H]a	*ak[H]
*k[ʌ]a	ak[ʌ]a	ak[ʌ]
g[H]a	ag[H]a	*ag[H]
g[ʌ]a	*ag[ʌ]a	ag[ʌ]

Of these combinations those marked * occur in E. The others require careful practice till they are familiar.

216. (g[ʌ]a) is easily obtained by pronouncing (aga), dwelling on the (g), and then dropping the initial (a). These 'full' initial voice-stops suggest the corresponding nasals to an unaccustomed ear, (d[ʌ]a), for instance, sounding like (na).

217. In forming (g[H]a) and (ag[H]a) be careful not to exaggerate the breath-glide, and in the latter not to separate it from the (g). (ag[H]a), and thence (g[H]a),

---

[a] The above details differ considerably from those of Mr. Ellis's latest views, as given in E. E. P. pp. 1097, 1111, &c. Mr. Ellis considers initial (g) to be always voiced, and that there is no necessary breath-glide after (k). He therefore identifies initial (g) with (g[ʌ]), and initial and medial (k) with (k[ʌ]), my initial (g).

may easily be obtained from the familiar (ag[ʜ]) by joining on an (a).

218. (ak[ʌ]a) is difficult for E. students. It can be formed by prefixing (a) to initial (ga-), although it is difficult to do so without making the stop voiced; or by trying to sound (aka) without any breath after the stop. These half-voice stops are the regular sounds of double *k*, *t*, and *p*, between vowels in Danish, as in (*i*k[ʌ]eh)= 'ikke,' (sæt[ʌ]eh)='sætte,' (d*y*p[ʌ]eh)='dyppe' [a].

219. There still remain final (ak[ʌ]) and (ag[ʌ]). The latter is easily formed, and is, in fact, sometimes heard in E. in such words as 'bigger' (b*i*g[ʌ]), when pronounced very rapidly. It is simply the influence of the spelling that makes us hear the final voice murmur as a separate syllable, even when it is reduced to its minimum. We also hear (b*i*g[ʌ]) as a dissyllable partly because the (g) is short, whereas the regular final (g) in 'big' is long, so that the 'dissyllable' (b*i*g[ʌ]) is actually shorter than the monosyllable (b*i*gɪ[ʜ]). If we lengthen the (g) of (b*i*g[ʌ]), making it into (b*i*gɪ[ʌ]), it has much more of a monosyllabic effect.

220. *On-glides.* The on-glide after a vowel is voiced in most languages (a[ʌ]k[ʜ]a), (a[ʌ]g[ʌ]a).

Voiceless on-glides occur in Icelandic regularly before double voiceless stops, as in (sæ[ʜ]tta)='setta,' (flo[ʜ]kka) ='flokka.' They may also be heard in Scotch, in such words as 'what' (who[ʜ]t).

Initial on-glides are, of course, inaudible when breathed.

---

[a] It appears now (Sievers, L. Ph. p. 64 foll.) that the S. German 'mediæ,' which were formerly assumed, on the authority of Brücke, to be 'whispered' consonants, are really these half-voiced stops. My own analysis of the Danish *kk* &c. was made some years ago, at a time when I still believed in the S. German whispered stops.

They may sometimes be heard voiced in such E. words as 'attempt' ([ʌ]tæmt), 'ago,' &c.

221. *Stress-glides* (Aspirated Stops). All stops, especially when voiceless, postulate a certain compression of the breath behind the stop, so as to produce an audible explosion when the stop is removed. On the force of this compréssion, which is caused by upward pressure of the diaphragm, the force of the glide and consequently the audibility of the stop mainly depend. The E. (k) &c. is generally pronounced with but little force, but in the German (k), as in 'kann,' there is a strong puff of breath, which may, however, be heard in E. as well in emphatic pronunciation.

222. But even in German the force of the breath-glide is something secondary, due only to the compression with which the stop is formed. If, however, a *separate* impulse is communicated to the glide, the glide is felt as an independent element. In this way the Irish and Danish 'aspirates' are formed, which are identical in sound, and entirely distinct from the German (k) in 'kann.' Examples are in Irish 'tell' (tʜælji), 'paper'; in Danish 'tale' (tʜɑ̨ɪleh), 'penge' (pʜæqeh), 'komme' (kʜɔmeh). These sounds have nothing harsh about them, their characteristic feature being the distinctness of their glide, which has something of the character of the preceding stop, so that (kʜa), for instance, sounds like a weak (kkha), &c. The analogies with the different vowel-beginnings (§ 195) are obvious.

223. It is also possible to substitute for the breath-glide an emission of breath through the fully opened glottis, with a separate impulse of breath, followed by a glide on to the vowel (kʜh[ʜ]a). This may be the one

form of aspiration in the modern Indian languages, which
has been described as making one imagine the speakers
were out of breath[a].

224. *Implosive Stops.* These Saxon German sounds were
first described by Merkel (Physiologie der Sprache, p. 149).
In Saxon German there is no distinction between *t* and *d*
&c., both being half-voiced (t[ʌ]), with the stop formed
implosively. The implosion consists in closing the glottis
simultaneously with the stop position, and then compressing the air between the glottis stoppage and the
mouth one, by raising the glottis like a plug by the action
of its muscles and by upward pressure of the diaphragm,
as in force generally. This action produces no sound
while the stop is being formed, but modifies the off-glide
in a very peculiar manner, giving it a 'choky' effect.

225. Sievers' description of the Tiflis Armenian and
Georgian implosives is very similar. He states that the
raising of the glottis is very energetic, amounting to fully
a half to three quarters of an inch[b].

UNSTOPPED CONSONANTS.

226. With unstopped consonants there is no difficulty
in voicing the stop itself, and there are many consonants,

---

[a] Quoted somewhere by Rumpelt (Natürliches System der Sprachlaute).

[b] The above details have been gathered partly from Merkel's
description, partly from Professor Sievers' pronunciation, who is
familiar with both the Saxon and the Armenian sounds. Sievers,
however, asserts that the Saxon implosives are not formed in the
same way as the Armenian, although he admits a certain similarity.
He thinks it possible that the Saxon implosives are formed by first
compressing the air in the mouth by the usual action of the diaphragm, and *then* closing the glottis.

especially the 'vowel-like' ones (§ 166), which are only occasionally devocalised. The glides of these consonants are always voiced as well.

227. In the breath unstopped consonants both the consonant itself and the off-glide are breathed, as in the corresponding stops: (s[н]a), (as[н]a), (as[н]). But the breath-glide of the unstopped consonants is always weaker than that of the stops, because the explosive effect of the latter is wanting.

228. Hence also the aspirates of these consonants are weaker and less marked than those of the stops, but they may be heard in the Irish 'sir,' and the Icelandic 'þaᵹ' (thнaιdh).

229. The voiced buzzes admit of more variety than the voiced stops, because with them the different stages of glottis-narrowing that may precede voice are distinctly audible, whereas in the voiced stop there is nothing between full vocality and absolute silence.

230. In medial (z), as in (aza), there can be no doubt of the vocality of the consonant, but initial and final (z) admit of various degrees of vocality.

(1) The glottis only begins to put itself in the position for voice when the (s) position is assumed, and consequently all the intermediate stages between full breath and full voice are heard in succession while the (s) position is being maintained. This is the 'gradual' initial (z), &c.

(2) The (z) is fully vocal throughout—that is, the glottis is closed for voice simultaneously with the beginning of the (z). This is the 'clear' initial (z).

It will be observed that these varieties of initial buzzes are exactly analogous to the two ways of beginning vowels (§ 195).

(3) The glottis is open during the formation of the consonant, and is only brought together at the moment when the off-glide begins. This is the 'half-voice' (z)= (s[ʌ]), corresponding to initial (ga-). As it is not easy to make the beginning of the voice correspond exactly with the beginning of the glide, this last variety is often modified into a compromise between (1) and (3), formed by beginning to narrow the glottis during the end of the consonant itself, so that the transition from breath to voice is completed just *before* beginning the glide.

231. If we compare these three varieties we find that they all agree in having voiced glides, and that in (2) the consonant itself is fully voiced, in (1) gradually voiced, and in (3) breathed.

232. The E. (z) in 'zeal' may be fully voiced, but is generally only gradually voiced. The half-voiced (z) seems to be the N. G. and Dutch initial (s), as in 'so,' 'zoo.' To an E. ear it sounds like (sz).

233. Final (z) may also be either fully vocalised throughout, or else gradually devocalised, passing from voice to whisper while the consonant position is still being maintained.

Both may be heard (but generally the latter) in the E. 'is,' &c. In final buzzes after other voice consonants the gradual devocalisation is very clearly marked in E. Thus in the final buzz in 'bills,' 'thieves,' 'adze,' &c., the vocality is of so short duration that the final (z) is almost a purely whispered consonant [a].

234. In this last case the glottis is not fully opened till the consonant is finished, which therefore consists of voice passing into whisper, followed by a breath-glide.

[a] Cp. § 236.

If the transition from voice to breath is completed during the beginning of the consonant itself, we have the Icelandic final (s), ' ís,' ' las,' &c., which sounds like (zs).

235. The vowel-like consonants when final occasionally end in a breath-glide. Thus, in pronouncing final (l) in Icelandic, the glottis opens just as the tongue is removed from the palate, making the resulting flap voiceless, as in ' vel' (veɪl[ʜ]), which sounds like (veɪl-lh). In French final (j) is pronounced in the same way, as in ' fille' (fij[ʜ]).

It is possible that in both these instances the glottis may be opened just *before* relaxing the consonant position.

Whispered Consonants.

236. Whisper being an intermediate stage between breath and whisper, is often generated as a secondary effect in the transition from one to the other. Thus the English *s* in ' heads' is distinctly whispered, although the beginning of it is voiced, together with the preceding (d). It seems, however, that the (z) may also be pronounced uniformly whispered throughout, in which case it must be regarded as a true whispered consonant (hedᶜz), in which the whisper is not merely something secondary.

In the case of stops the whisper is inaudible in the stop itself, and is only heard in the glide. In most cases a whispered glide would be felt as a transition to or from voice, and would therefore have simply the effect of a weak breath-glide. Indeed, it is very probable that the breath-glide in (k[ʜ]a) and (ag[ʜ]) may often be really (k[ˈʌ]a) and (ag[ˈʌ]), or rather consist of both, the one gliding insensibly into the other.

(ak[ˈʌ]), on the other hand, is distinguishable from

(ak[н]), and this seems to be the pronunciation of final *gg, dd, bb* in Icelandic, as in 'egg' (æ'gɪ).

OTHER MODIFICATIONS OF CONSONANT-GLIDES.

237. We have hitherto considered consonant glides as modified mainly by voice, breath, and force. But they are capable of other modifications. Thus, if during the formation of a (k)-stop the lips are brought into the (ph) or (wh) position, the off-glide will assume a distinctly labial or labio-guttural character (k[нʊ]a), which, although not very marked, is distinctly audible. If this (k[нʊ]a) is made into an aspirate we obtain (kнʊa). The former occurs in the E. 'cool,' the latter in the Danish 'kunde' (kнʊo'neh), in both cases with cheek-narrowing as well, the rounding of the glide being nothing but an anticipation of the position of the following vowel.

238. In the same way the off-glide in (ta) may be gutturalised or palatalised and modified in various other ways.

These effects are mostly due to assimilation, and therefore of a secondary character.

GLIDELESS COMBINATIONS.

239. The consistent application of the principle already enunciated, namely that in passing from one sound to another the shortest way is taken, occasionally results in combinations which are effected without any glide at all. Such combinations are impossible in the case of vowels, but are frequent in that of a sequence of consonants formed in the same place and differing only

in form. Thus, if a nasal is followed by the corresponding voice stop, as in (nd), all that is required to pass from
one to the other is simply to close the nasal passage.
Similarly, in the combination (dl) the transition is made by
simply opening the side apertures, the tip of the tongue
retaining its position. In such cases the absence of glides,
the 'glideless transition,' is implied by the juxtaposition
of the elements of the combination, just as a glide is
necessarily implied by the juxtaposition of two vowels.

240. Combinations such as (ts), (tsh), (pph), (pf), &c.,
in which a stop is followed by open consonants formed in
the same, or nearly the same, place, are either absolutely
glideless, as in the case of (pph) or (ts) when the (t) is a
blade-stop, or the glide is so insignificant as to be practically non-existent, as in the case of (tsh). These combinations are very similar in sound to the simple aspirates
(tH), (pH), &c., and the open consonants may almost be
regarded as substitutes for the breath-glide—we might, in
short, define (ppha) as (p) gliding on to (a) through the
(ph) position, were it not that the (ph) has a definite configuration, which, although extremely short, is held for a
moment.

241. Even when consonants formed in different places
come together it is possible to combine them without any
glide, although in this case the gliding combination must
be regarded as the normal form. Thus the transition
from (k) to (t) in (akta) is effected by removing the back
of the tongue from the (k) position and then forming the
(t) position with the point, so that there is an audible
breath-glide (ak[H]ta). The Swedish (akta) is pronounced
in this way, and the same pronunciation is the regular
one in French. In English, on the other hand, there is

no glide whatever, the tip of the tongue being brought into position before the (k) contact is loosened, so that the stoppage of the mouth passage is maintained from the beginning of the (k) to the end of the (t): all that is heard, therefore, is the on-glide of the (k) and the off-glide of the (t). All combinations of consonants are effected in this way in English and many other languages —probably in most, the glide being either entirely omitted, or else reduced to practical inaudibility. Thus (k) and (l) are joined together in English in exactly the same way as (k) and (t), while in (lk) the (k) position is assumed so immediately after the (l) that the glide is reduced to practically nothing at all. The difference between (kl) and (lk) is that in (kl) the (l) can assume its position simultaneously with the (k) without modifying its sound, whereas the stop (k) would at once destroy the sound of (l).

242. There are, however, many fine distinctions to be observed in language. Thus in the Dutch ' volk ' there is a distinct voice-glide from the (l) to the (k), which gives the word something of a dissyllabic effect. Initial (kn) in German, as in 'knie,' is often (k[H]n), with a distinct breath-glide, while in Danish there is no glide ; and as initial voiceless stops are aspirated in Danish (kHn) becomes (knh), as in (knh*ee*x)='knæ,' (nh) being substituted for the simple breath-glide.

GLIDE CONSONANTS.

243. A glide consonant is one which is only heard in its transition to or from another element, the consonant itself being either not formed at all, or made inaudible by want of breath.

244. Thus the peculiar Japanese (r) seems to be
formed by first bringing the tip of the tongue against the
gums without any emission of breath, and then passing on
to an untrilled (r), allowing voiced breath to pass at the
moment of removing the tongue. As Mr. Ellis remarks [a],
the Japanese 'seem unable to pronounce (r) without
striking the palate first.' This (r) may be represented by
([d]r) or ([l]r). An unaccustomed ear hears it as something between (r), (l), and (d). The Japanese pronounce
all foreign (l)s and (r)s as this sound, so that when a
Japanese says 'a little man,' it sounds to an English ear
like 'a literal man.'

245. In English, when a stop follows a vowel, the
breath impulse is often so feeble that nothing is heard but
part of the glide on to the consonant, the actual closure
being formed without any breath at all. Thus (b*i*gɪ) becomes (b*i*[g̊]). With nasals (mænɪ) becomes (mæ[ʌ*n*]),
only a nasal glide being audible.

[a] Ellis, E. E. P. p. 1133

GENERAL SYNTHESIS.

We have hitherto considered the synthesis of special combinations of sounds ; there now remain those laws of synthesis that apply to combined sounds generally.

246. The popular fourfold division of the elements of speech into letters (that is, sounds), syllables, words, and sentences, is not purely phonetic, but also partly graphical and logical. The first and most important point is to see clearly that our ordinary word-division is a logical and not a phonetic analysis. No amount of study of the sounds only of a sentence will enable us to recognise the individual words of which it consists. We may write down every sound, every shade of synthesis, but we shall never be able to analyse it into separate words till we know its meaning, and even then we shall find that word-division postulates much thought and comparison of sentences one with another. The fixity of our conventional word-division and the mechanical way in which we learn it blinds us to the real complexity of the questions involved in it, and to the fact that there is no word-division whatever in language itself, considered simply as an aggregate of sounds.

247. The only division actually made in language is that into ' breath-groups.' We are unable to utter more than a certain number of sounds in succession, without renewing the stock of air in the lungs. These breath-groups correspond partially with the logical division into sentences: every sentence is necessarily a breath-group, but every breath-group need not be a complete sentence.

248. Within each breath-group there is no pause whatever, and the popular idea that we make a pause after every word is quite false. Thus, in such a sentence as ' put on your hat,' we hear clearly the final breath-glide, the ' recoil,' as it is sometimes called, which follows the final (t) of ' hat,' but the (t) of ' put ' runs its glide on to the following vowel exactly as in the single word ' putting,' and there is no recoil. In ' put back ' there is no glide at all after the (t) [a].

249. The other phonetic divisions, of word and syllable, are clearly the result of deliberate analysis. The discrimination of the separate sounds of language is the problem we have been working at in the analytical section of this work. There remains therefore the difficult question of syllable-division.

SYLLABLE DIVISION.

250. The audibility of language depends mainly on its vowels. It would be easy enough to construct a language composed entirely of consonants, but such a language would be inaudible except at very short distances. Acoustically speaking, consonants are mere modifiers of the vowels, and the ideal of distinctness would be reached by a language in which each consonant was separated from the next by a vowel.

251. Hence the ear soon learns to divide the sentences (breath-groups) of language into groups of vowels, each

[a] Cp. § 241.

vowel being flanked by subordinate consonants. The analysis into separate consonants is a later one, as proved by the universal priority of syllabic over single-letter alphabets.

252. It often happens that a vowel-like consonant takes the place of a vowel, or rather of a vowel and a consonant. Thus in English (li̇tl) = ' little ' suggests (l) + the neutral vowel (li̇tehl). In such a word as the Bohemian (kghrk) there is no vowel at all.

253. Some of the breath-sibilants are audible enough in themselves, and there are several interjectional words in which they have a distinctly vowel-effect. Thus (shɪ) by itself is used, and in combination with stops (sɪt) and (psɪt), &c. The want of vocality, however, makes the ear somewhat unwilling to recognise the syllabic value of these consonants. The influence of voice in giving syllabic effect is strikingly shown in the stops with final voice glide (§ 219).

254. It often happens that when two vowel-like consonants come together, one is regarded as a vowel (with a consonant), the other as a consonant. As a general rule the one that has the greater force (stress) and is the longest is felt to contain the vowel. Thus (mn·)ᵃ suggest (m-ehn), and (m·n) (ehm-n)ᵇ

255. We see, then, that the conception of a syllable is necessarily a somewhat vague one, which may vary in different languages, and may also be partly dependent on the associations of the written language.

The question now arises, where does each syllable begin?

ᵃ The (·) indicates stress, beginning on the preceding sound.
ᵇ Compare Sievers, L. Ph. p. 26 foll.

256. As we have seen (§ 184), the sense of unity is mainly due to continuity of force. If sentences were uttered with level force throughout, the question of syllable-division could not be raised at all : we should be able to count the number of vowels, and thus determine the number of syllables, but we should never be able to settle where one syllable left off and another began, unless we adopted purely arbitrary criteria.

257. We find, however, that the different syllables of which any sound-group is composed are uttered with various degrees of force. This relative force of syllables is called 'stress' or 'accent.' For the present it is enough to distinguish between weak and strong accent, marking the latter by a (ˑ) after the sound on which the stress begins. We have already seen that the strength of each separate force-impulse, such as we give to the separate syllables of any sound-group, tends to diminish progressively, until a new impulse begins, which in its turn diminishes progressively. The beginning of each of these force-impulses marks the beginning of the syllable. Thus the two sound-groups (ʌnˑeiɩhm) and (ʌneˑɩɩhm) differ solely in the place where the stress begins, but their meaning is totally distinct, the first signifying 'a name,' the second 'an aim.' In the first the stress, and consequently the syllable, begins on the (n), in the second on the vowel. Similarly (ʌtˑrehɩh)='a try,' (ʌtrˑehɩh)='at Rye,' (ʌtɔɩˑltˑehɩhmz)='at all times,' (ʌtˑɔɩlmˑæn)='a tall man.'

258. We see from these examples that the beginning of syllables is partly indicated by the ordinary word-division, that is, in all cases where a word happens to begin on a syllable with a strong stress. If a word begins

on a weak-stressed syllable the beginning of its strong
syllable is not indicated, thus 'attack' might be either
(ʌt·æk), which is the actual pronunciation, or (ʌtæ·k),
which would suggest 'at Ack.' Similarly, if we were
to write 'atall' in one word, it might be pronounced
either (ʌt·ɔɪl) or (ʌtɔ·ɪl). In 'at all,' when used as an
adverb, as in 'not at all' (and 'at home,' as generally
pronounced), the word-division does not indicate the
true syllabification, which is (ʌt·ɔɪl) in ordinary speech.

259. The only phonetic function of word-division is,
therefore, to indicate occasionally the syllable-divisions
in sentences.

260. It must be noted that syllabification depends not
on mere force, but on discontinuity of force. Thus in
'ticket' and 'take it' the syllabification is exactly the
same, the (k) belonging to the first syllable in both
groups, and although the (k) is pronounced stronger
in 'ticket' than in 'take it' it does not therefore begin
a new syllable. In both cases the (k) is uttered with part
of the same force-impulse as the preceding vowel, and the
difference in force of the two (k)s is simply due to the
different lengths of the two vowels (§ 183). To make (k)
in 'ticket' the beginning of the second syllable, it would
be necessary to diminish the force of the (ti) very rapidly,
so as to be able to begin a fresh impulse of force on
the (k); nor need this impulse be strong—only just
enough to break the continuity of the force decrease [a].
If the (k) and the following vowel are pronounced with

---

[a] In this way are pronounced the short Swiss German vowels
before single consonants, as in *gebe*, *lese* (Sievers, L. Ph. 116). This
Swiss syllabification is best acquired by shortening the usual long
gebe without increasing the force of the *b* (which is (p[ʌ])): see
§ 218).

a stronger force-impulse than the (t*i*), the syllabification and the stress are both changed, (t·*i*k-*i*t) becoming (t*i*-k·*i*t).

261. The distinction between long and double consonants is purely syllabic. In (a·tɪa), (a·lɪa), the consonant positions are simply held with uniformly diminishing force until the (a) is reached, on which a new impulse begins. In (atta) (alla) the consonants are held as long as in the former cases, but the new force-impulse begins in the second half of the held consonants, without waiting till the vowel is reached, which, of course, breaks the sense of continuity.

262. The distinction between 'cut short' (kɐtsh·ɔɪt) and 'achieve' (ʌt·shiɪv), 'outside' (æhohts·ehɪhd) and the German 'geziemen' (geht·sɪɪmehn), is exactly analogous.

STRESS.

263. We have already defined stress (accent) as the comparative force with which the separate syllables of a sound-group are pronounced. In speaking of the stress of a sentence as opposed to that of single words the term 'emphasis' is used, but there is no *phonetic* distinction, which is one of *meaning* only.

264. For practical purposes it is enough to discriminate three degrees of stress, weak, medium (secondary), strong. The weak stress is left unmarked, the strong is indicated by a (·) after the symbol of the stress element, and the medium by (:). 'Very strong' may be expressed by (··).

265. The variations of stress are infinite, and in a single sound-group (word or sentence), every syllable

may have a different degree of stress. Thus, such a
word as 'impenetrability' has, roughly speaking, two
stresses, one strong one on the fifth, and a medium one
on the first [a]. But if we pronounce 'bility' by itself we
shall find that all three syllables have a different stress,
the third being stronger than the second, and yet, of
course, weaker than the first. In 'penetra' there is the
same relation, but all the syllables are a shade weaker
than the corresponding ones in 'bility.' The order of
the syllables in stress is therefore as follows, 1 being
the highest :—

$$\begin{array}{ccccccc} 2 & 3 & 7 & 5 & 1 & 6 & 4 \end{array}$$
im - pe - ne - tra - bi   li - ty.

266. The surest way of determining the relative force
of any two syllables is to pronounce the other syllables
mentally only, or in a whisper, pronouncing the special
syllables aloud, and their relative force will then come
out clearly. Thus, taking 'bility' by itself, if we utter
the first syllable mentally, the other two aloud, we shall
hear that the second of them has the stronger stress.

267. There is an important feature of stress generally,
which in most cases makes any minuter symbolisation
of stress unnecessary. This is its *rhythmic* character,
or the tendency to alternate weak and strong stress.
Perfect uniformity of stress is as unnatural as level force
in the separate syllables would be, but the tendency of
stress is not, like that of a single force impulse, to
decrease progressively, but rather to sway to and fro.
Hence, if we have a group of three syllables, the first
of which has the predominant stress, we may generally

----

[a] Often on the second instead.

infer that the second will be weaker than the third, unless special modifications intervene.

268. To discriminate degrees of stress is no easy matter, and requires considerable training, especially when there are counter-distinctions of quantity, tone, &c. The student should carefully practise himself in analysing the stress, first in words, where it is fixed, and then in short natural sentences, where it is not fixed, but otherwise follows the same laws as in words; sentences, as well as words, always having one predominant stress, which gives the whole group a character of unity.

269. The distinctions of stress in some languages are less marked than in others. Thus in French the syllables are all pronounced with a nearly uniform stress, the strong syllables rising only a little above the general level, its occurrence being also uncertain and fluctuating. This makes Frenchmen unable without systematic training to master the accentuation of foreign languages.

TONES AND PITCH [a].

270. Variations of pitch (or tone) depend, as already remarked, on the rapidity of the sound-vibrations, which again depend on the length of the vocal chords.

271. Changes of tones may proceed either by leaps or glides. In singing the voice dwells without change of pitch on each note, and leaps upwards or downwards to the next note as quickly as possible, so that although

---

[a] The best treatment of this subject will be found in Mr. Bell's 'Elocutionary Manual.'

there is no break, the intermediate 'glide-tone' is not noticed. In speech the voice only occasionally dwells on one note, but is constantly moving upwards or downwards from one note to the other, so that the different notes are simply points between which the voice is constantly gliding.

272. There are, therefore, three primary 'forms' or 'inflections' of tones :—

level   –

rising /

falling \

273. The level tone may be heard in 'well,' as an expression of musing or meditation; the rising in questions or doubtful statements; the falling in answers, commands, or dogmatic assertions.

274. It is also possible to have level tones connected by intermediate glide-tones, as in the 'portamento' in singing.

275. Besides the simple rise and fall, there are compound tones, formed by uniting both in one syllable :—

the compound rising v

   „   „   falling ʌ

276. v may be heard in such a sentence as 'take care!' when uttered warningly; ʌ in 'oh!' 'oh really,' when implying sarcasm. These tones are, however, best learnt by combining their elements.

277. It is possible to combine three tones in one syllable. Thus we can have ʌ followed by /, which has the effect of v, only somewhat more emphatic.

278. All these tones can be varied indefinitely according to the interval through which they pass. As a

general rule, the greater the interval the more marked
the character of the tone. Thus, a rise through a small
interval (a second for instance) denotes mere enquiry,
through a large one (such as a sixth) surprise. Again,
the semitone (minor) interval has a plaintive effect, but
here the less the interval the more marked its minor
character, most of all therefore in the simple semitone
or half-tone. The reason of this is that sadness, like
all un-energetic emotions, naturally expresses itself in
inflections of narrow range.

279. The whole relation of tone to language has as
yet been only imperfectly studied, and all that can be
expected from the student in our present state of knowledge is the power of discriminating the four inflections
/, \, ∧, and ∧.

280. The use of tones varies greatly in different languages. In English the tones express various logical
and emotional modifications, such as surprise, uncertainty, &c. In some languages there is a tendency to
employ one predominant tone without much regard to
its meaning. Thus in Scotch the rising tone is often
employed monotonously, not only in questions but also
in answers and statements of facts. In Glasgow Scotch
the falling tone predominates. In American English the
compound rise is the characteristic tone.

281. In all these cases the tones are functionally
'sentence-tones,' that is, they modify the general meaning
of the whole sentence. In some languages, however,
such as Swedish, Lithuanian, Chinese, Siamese, and the
Indo-Chinese family generally, each word has its own
special tone (rising, falling, &c.), which is as much an
integral part of it as the sounds of which it is composed,

and does not, therefore, vary with the general sense of the sentence.   This tone may be called 'word-tone.'

282. Besides the separate inflections of which it is composed, each sentence, or sentence-group, has a general pitch, or 'key' of its own.

283. For ordinary purposes it is enough to distinguish three representative keys—

high ⌐

middle ⌐∟

low ∟

284. The middle key may also be left unmarked. The high key is natural in all strong and joyful emotions, the low in sadness and solemnity.

285. Change of key has often a purely logical significance.   Thus questions are naturally uttered in a higher key than answers, and parenthetic clauses in a lower key than those which state the main facts.   In all natural speech there is incessant change of key.

286. Changes of key may proceed either by leaps or progressively.   Progressive change of key is indicated by prefixing ⁄ or ＼ to the signs of key-change.   Thus ⁄⌐ is heard in all cases of passion increasing to a climax.

Connection between Force, Quantity, and Pitch.

287. There is a natural connection between force, length, and high pitch, and conversely between weak force, shortness, and low pitch.

288. The connection between force and pitch is especially intimate.   All energetic emotions naturally express themselves in high tones and forcible utterance, and increased vehemence of emotion is always accompanied by a rise in force and pitch.

289. The association of force and quantity is less intimate. There is, however, a natural tendency to pass over the less important unaccented elements of speech, and to dwell on the prominent stress-syllables, whence that shortening of unaccented long, and lengthening of accented short syllables which is so common in modern languages.

290. It is, however, an entire mistake to suppose that these natural tendencies represent necessities, and that high tone and strong stress can be regarded as convertible terms. Just as on the piano the lowest note in the bass can be struck with the same force as the highest one in the treble, so in language it often happens that strong stress is combined with low pitch, and vice-versa. Still less can quantity be identified with stress.

VOICE-QUALITY (TIMBRE).

291. Besides the various modifications of stress, tone, &c., the quality of the voice may be modified through whole sentences by various glottal, pharyngal, and oral influences.

292. The most important are those known as the 'clear' and the 'dull' qualities of the voice. The latter is due to lateral compression, the former to its absence. There are, of course, various intermediate degrees, and the dull quality may be exaggerated by cheek and lip rounding, as we hear in the pronunciation of those badly-

I

trained singers who make (a) nearly into (*o*) on a high note. This exaggerated dulling of the voice may also be heard as an individual peculiarity, giving what is commonly called a 'sepulchral' tone. The dull quality is the natural expression of sadness, solemnity, or tenderness, and is so employed instinctively in natural speech and in singing.

Among the many other varieties of voice quality, which are mostly individual or national peculiarities, the following may be noticed :—

293. Narrowing of the upper glottis (ʀ) gives an effect of strangulation. It is common among Scotchmen, and combined with high key gives the pronunciation of the Saxon Germans its peculiarly harsh character.

294. Partial closure of the mouth is a common English peculiarity. It has a tendency to labialise back vowels, and even where there is not actual labialisation it gives the vowels generally a muffled sound, so that (*a*), for instance, is not easily distinguished from (*ɔ*). It also tends to make the general speech nasal, for the breath being impeded in its passage through the mouth, naturally seeks another through the nose. Germans sometimes say of the English, with humorous exaggeration, that they speak, not with their mouth like other people, but with their nose and throat.

295. Lip-influence is very important. General lip contraction is a natural accompaniment of partial mouth closure and nasality, also of the dull quality of the voice. Conversely, the clear quality may be made more decided by spreading out the corners of the mouth, as in the pronunciation of (i). This is frequently employed by singers to give a laughing effect. In many languages, such as French and many Scotch dialects, the lips are often protruded in forming rounded sounds, while in others, such as English, the lips are not employed more than is necessary, inner rounding being chiefly relied on.

296. These modifications must be carefully distinguished from those which are due to peculiarities in the organs of speech themselves. Thus defects in the palate may cause permanent nasality (together with a peculiar hollowness of sound), an abnormally large tongue gutturality, &c. All of these peculiarities are inseparable from the individual.

PART IV.

SOUND-NOTATION.

297. THE notation of sounds is scarcely less important than their analysis : without a clear and consistent system of notation it is impossible to discuss phonetic questions intelligibly or to describe the phonetic structure of a language.

298. The only perfect alphabet would evidently be one in which every symbol bore a definite relation to the sound it represented. In the Roman alphabet these relations are entirely arbitrary, and an alphabet that has any claim to the title of 'rational' must therefore discard the Roman letters entirely. In Mr. Bell's 'Visible Speech,' accordingly, an entirely new set of symbols is used, which indicate the action of the organs in every case, all the symbols being made up of a few simple elements, which can be combined to any extent. If the phonetic analysis on which Visible Speech is based were perfect, the alphabet itself might, with a few alterations, easily be made practically perfect, and capable of representing all possible sounds whatever with the minutest accuracy. But until phonetics are in a much more advanced state than they are at present, Visible Speech cannot be considered secure against the necessity of incessant alteration and correction.

299. The Roman alphabet, on the other hand, not being based on a phonetic analysis, is not liable to be disturbed by any new discoveries. It has also the great advantage of having long been in practical use both in printing and writing.

300. The imperfections of the Roman alphabet may be remedied in four ways :

(1) by casting new types;

(2) by employing diacritics, such as grave and acute accents, &c.;

(3) by employing digraphs, such as *th, kh,* &c. ;

(4) by employing turned letters, italics and capitals.

The same objection applies both to (1) and (2), when carried out to any extent, namely that a new system should utilise the means already existing before creating new ones, which involve expense and inconvenience of all kinds; and if we are to cast new types, it would be simplest to discard the Roman alphabet altogether, and take a simplified form of Visible Speech, which would certainly be far easier to learn and use than any possible modification of the Roman alphabet. The practical experience of Mr. Ellis is decisive on this point. He entirely discards such systems as Pitman's 'Phonotypy,' and Lepsius's 'Standard Alphabet,' the best known representatives of (1) and (2), and falls back entirely on (3) and (4), which employ only the ordinary resources of the printing-office. That it is possible with such means as these to form a practicable system, Mr. Ellis has clearly shown in his 'Palæotype.'

301. The great defect of Palæotype, and the other

systems contrived by Mr. Ellis, is their unnecessary arbitrariness, especially in the vowels, which makes his symbols extremely difficult to remember [a].

In the present work a new system has therefore been constructed, in which the greatest possible regularity and consistency has been aimed at, as far as the radical defects of the Roman alphabet allow. Those who know palæotype will easily see how principles partly developed by Mr. Ellis have been carried out consistently as far as possible.

302. Another defect of palæotype is the multiplicity of signs employed. Mr. Ellis's principle of attempting to find a symbol for every sound that is possible, or has been described by others, seems out of place in any adaptation of the Roman alphabet, which can only be a temporary compromise. All that is necessary is to find signs for the fundamental distinctions, and the minuter or exceptional ones can easily be supplied by simple description. Thus if the reader is once told that the Danish (o) is formed by abnormal rounding (§ 42), he simply has to remember this whenever he comes across a Danish word with (o) in it. If attention is to be specially called to any peculiarity, this can easily be done by putting a * after the symbol, to remind the reader that some modifier is understood.

303. This system, which I call 'Romic' (because based on the original Roman values of the letters),

---

[a] The most striking instance of this arbitrariness is the use of (e) to denote the wide, while (o) denotes the narrow sound of the two vowels. The parallelism of these two sounds is thus entirely destroyed, which, as far as I know, is not the case in any other system, even the clumsiest.

although probably the simplest possible for an accurate analysis of sounds generally, is too cumbersome as well as too minute for many practical purposes [a]. In treating the relations of sounds without going into minute details, and in giving passages of any length in phonetic writing, and especially in dealing with a limited number of sounds, as in treating of a single language, it is necessary to have an alphabet which indicates only those broader distinctions of sound which actually correspond to distinctions of meaning in language, and indicates them by letters which can be easily written and remembered.

304. Thus, the innumerable varieties of diphthongs possible can all be classed under a few general categories such as (ai), (au), (oi) diphthongs, and if we simply provide unambiguous signs for these general categories, we can ignore the endless shades of difference within them, because these differences do not alter the meaning or application of the words in which they occur. Again, even if we confine our attention to definite distinctions, such as those of narrow and wide, close (e) and open (æ) &c., which *may* correspond to differences of meaning, we find that each language utilises only a few of these distinctions. Thus, in English, there is no distinction between narrow and wide in short vowels, most short vowels being wide only, while in French (i) and (u) are always narrow both long and short, (*i*) and (*u*) being unknown. In Danish, on the other hand, short (i) and (*i*) often distinguish words which would otherwise be

---

[a] This cumbrousness is inseparable from any attempts at extension of the radically defective Roman alphabet. In Visible Speech, on the other hand, the most minute synthetic distinctions can be symbolised without causing the slightest practical inconvenience.

identical. Icelandic only has (i) when short, but separates
(iɪ) and (ɪ) when long, often distinguishing words solely
by the narrowness or wideness of the vowel. Danish has
(iɪ) only when long, as in English also. We see from
this that the distinction between (i) and (ɪ) is a *significant*
one in Danish and Icelandic ; that is, one that corresponds to real distinctions in the languages themselves,
while in French it does not exist at all. In English there
is the distinction, but it is not an *independent* one, being
associated with quantity. But to write (iɪ), (ɪ) in English
would be superfluous, as length and narrowness, shortness
and wideness go together, and if we simply write (iɪ) and
(i) the quantity would always *imply* the distinctions of
narrow and wide. Hence we may lay down as a general
rule that only those distinctions of sounds require to be
symbolised in any one language which are *independently
significant :* if two criteria of significance are inseparably
associated, such as quantity and narrowness or wideness,
we only need indicate one of them.

305. What is wanted then is a general system which is
capable of being modified on definite principles to suit the
requirements of special languages. This general system
should, of course, deviate as little as possible from the
scientific one, and should be as little arbitrary as possible
in its details. Like the scientific system it should be
based on the original Roman values of the letters [a],
supplemented by digraphs and turned letters.

306. Beginning, then, with the vowels, there is no
difficulty in determining the general application of the
elementary symbols *a, æ, e, i, o, œ* (=Fr. '*peur*'), *u, y*
(=Fr. *u*), but signs are required for the *u* in '*but*' and

---

[a] See my 'History of English Sounds,' pp. 21 foll.

the allied back and mixed vowels, the close French *eu* in
' peu,' and the 'open' *o*. For the open *o*, and for French
eu, we can have little hesitation in adopting the ɔ and ə of
the other system, and ə may be extended to the English
u in 'but' and 'burn,' and the German *e* in 'gabe,' &c.

307. The following will then be the different values of
each of the vowel signs in this system, which I will call
' Broad Romic,' in apposition to the scientific ' Narrow
Romic,' as indicating only *broad* distinctions of sound.

$$a = a, a.$$
$$æ = e, æ, æ.$$
$$e = e.$$
$$ə = v, ɐ, ʋ; eh, \&c.; ə.$$
$$i = i, i.$$
$$o = o, oh, oh.$$
$$ɔ = o, ɔ, ɔ, ɔh, \&c.$$
$$œ = ə, œ, œ.$$
$$u = u, u, uh, uh.$$
$$y = y, y.$$

The diphthongs are expressed by *ai, au, oi, œi,* &c.,
minuter shades being disregarded. Long vowels are
doubled. Broad Romic words or passages are written in
italics or distinguished by (' '), not inclosed in ( ).

308. The consonant symbols will be the same as in
Narrow Romic, except that all capitals are discarded, the
front consonants being indicated by *j*, thus—*lj, njh,* &c.
The superfluous letters *c* and *x* will be employed as
convenient abbreviations of digraphs in each language.
Thus in English *c* may be used for *tsh*, in German for
kh, in French for *sh*, and so on. Any letter which
happens not to have a sound to represent in any language

will be employed in the same way. Thus the vowel *y* is superfluous in English, and may, therefore, be used to represent the sound (j), *j* itself denoting *dzh*, parallel to *c* = *tsh*.

309. To prevent confusion in comparing different languages, it will often be advisable either to substitute the full spellings (tsh), &c., for the contracted ones, or else to print the letters that are used in special senses in italics. Thus ' va*r* ' in Danish would remind the reader that the Danish *r* is not the ordinary *r*, but a laryngal sound.

310. Whenever the ' broad ' symbols are inadequate it is, of course, allowable to take others from the ' narrow ' system. Thus *ih* = (ih) might be employed in Welsh, and (ʀ) might be introduced into Danish for special purposes. Capitals and italics, however, being inconvenient in rapid writing, it is best to form special combinations when such distinctions as those of narrow and wide are required, which is very seldom the case. Thus the wide (i) may be expressed by *ie*, as being intermediate in sound to (i) and (e).

311. The main principle to be observed in all these contrivances is not to disturb the general associations of the letters more than is necessary, and never to lose sight of the importance of keeping up the international character of both the Narrow and the Broad system.

312. There now remains the question of synthesis-notation. After what has been said on the phonetic value of word-division (§ 246) no surprise need be felt at finding its abandonment advocated here. But, as I have remarked elsewhere [a], the abandonment of conven-

---

[a] In a paper on ' Words, Logic, and Grammar,' Trans. of Philological Society, 1876.

tional word-division by no means implies writing each sentence as an unbroken whole. We have already seen (§ 258) that word-division serves, whenever it has any phonetic meaning at all, to indicate stress-division. If, then, we carry out this principle consistently, making each letter-division correspond with the beginning of a strong stress, as in (henɾe¹ keɾ*i*hm hoɪo¹m jestʌde¹), we shall indicate the most important synthetical element of speech in the simplest and clearest way possible. The (·) otherwise required to mark the strong stress, will thus be available for the medium (secondary) stresses in each sound-group, as in (tuɪw kænʌnbˑɔɪlz), while, if placed at the beginning of a group, it will indicate very strong stress, the ordinary strong stress being implied by simple division, and weak stress by non-division. The (:) thus becomes quite superfluous, and four degrees of stress are expressed by a single sign. When a sound-group begins, as is often the case, on a weak stress, a special mark is required. The most convenient one is (–), as in (–dhʌ mænɪdhʌteh*i*h sɔɪ). When the sound-group begins on a secondary stress, (:) may be prefixed, as in (:kɐm ɐp), instead of (–) followed by (·), which would otherwise be required.

313. Tone would be indicated by –, ⁄ and \, &c., which would take the place of the ordinary marks of punctuation at the end of each breath-group, thus serving the double purpose of indicating breath-division and intonation. Marks of key, voice-quality, &c., would be prefixed to each group. There are of course various degrees of accuracy required for different purposes. For the purely practical applications of Broad-sign mere-stress divisions, with an occasional use of (·) when necessary, together

with the simple tone-marks, are amply sufficient, and the
(–) may be omitted whenever the syllable to which it is
prefixed is one whose phonetic structure does not allow it
to take a strong stress; thus, in 'rə təən' = *return*, we
see at once that 'rə' cannot be an accented syllable
because of the final 'ə.'

314. Whenever word-division is indicated it must be
understood to be something altogether extraneous and
subordinate, just like indicating the substantives in German
by capitals.   Word-division is perfectly useless to those
readers who are practically familiar with the particular
language: they do not hear any word-division in rapid
speech, and require it still less in slow deliberate reading.
Whenever word-division is required it can easily be
indicated in Broad Romic by italics or capitals, which
otherwise are not employed at all.

SPECIMENS.

ENGLISH.

THE following table will give an idea of the relations of the English vowels to the general scheme.

		i(j)		ih	i
ɐ		e(ih)	aɪ	eh(ih)	e
	æhɪ	æɪ		æh(ʌw)	æ
u(w)			u		
o[oʲ]			o(ih)		
ɔɪ			ɔ		

Voice-glide (ʌ). Voice-glide-round (ʌw).

The following list shows the correspondence of the Broad Romic letters, with examples:—

aa	= (aɪ)	*as in*	father.
æ	= (æ)	,,	had.
ae	= (æɪ)	,,	hair.
ai	= (ehih)	,,	fly.
ao	= (ɔɪ)	,,	fall.
au	= (æhʌw)	,,	now.
c	= (e), (æ), (ih)[a]	,,	head, ready.

[a] Only in unaccented syllables (except in a very few instances).

ei	= (e*i*h)	*as in*	fa*i*l.
ə	= (ɐ), (ʌ)[a]	„	b*u*d, bett*er*.
əə	= (æhi)	„	b*ir*d.
i	= (*i*)	„	f*i*ll.
ii, iy	= (iɪ), (ij)	„	f*ee*l.
o	= (ɔ), (ʌ*w*)[a]	„	f*o*lly, foll*ow*.
oi	= (o*i*h)	„	b*oy*.
ou	= (oo¹)	„	n*o*.
u	= (*u*)	„	f*u*ll.
uu, uw	= (uɪ), (uw)	„	f*oo*l.

In English B. R. *ae* and *ao* are used instead of *æəæ* and *ɔɔ*, as being more convenient to write, and as symplifying the system by enabling us to dispense with *ə* altogether. *æəæ* and *ɔɔ* may, however, be employed for special comparisons.

The narrowness of all E. vowels is uncertain, especially the diphthongs (ij), (e*i*h), (uw), and (oo¹), which may all be pronounced wide, although they seem generally to be intermediate between narrow and wide. The narrowness of (e*i*h) is especially doubtful. (ij) is generally fully widened before (r) or its weakening (ʌ), and often becomes monophthongic, (h*i*ɪʌ) = 'here.' (eh*i*h), (æhʌ*w*), and (o*i*h) seem to be always fully wide. (ɐ), (æhɪ), and (ɔɪ) seem generally to preserve their narrowness, especially (ɔɪ). (æ) is never widened into (*æ*), although it often interchanges with (*e*) by imitation.

As regards position, (*i*) is often lowered, and regularly becomes (*e*¹) in unaccented syllables, which before consonants, as in 'fish*e*s,' interchanges with (*i*h). (*i*h) is not uncommon in accented syllables also in careless speech,

---

[a] Only in unaccented syllables.

and is especially common in certain words, such as
'pretty' (pri*h*te¹), 'just' as an adverb, as in 'j*u*st so.' (*i*h)
seems to preponderate over (e¹) in rapid and careless
speech. It is, however, difficult to separate them with
certainty, for (e¹) naturally passes into (*i*h), if raised a
little while the front of the tongue is kept down, and not
allowed to rise quite into the (*i*) position.

The position of (ɔ) is often raised towards (o), which it
generally reaches in the diphthong (o*i*h).

All the back vowels are liable to be advanced towards
the mixed positions, especially (uw) and (*u*), which often
closely resemble the Swedish *u*.

The only unaccented vowels in E. are (e¹) and (*i*h) and
(ʌ) and (ʌ*w*)[a].

The second elements of the diphthongs which start
from low or mid vowels all have a tendency towards (ʌ),
hence (o*i*h) often becomes (oʌ) or perhaps (oˌʌ). In (ij)
the (j) appears to be often narrow, and when the (*i*) is
wide the sound seems to be often (*i*[i]) with the (*i*) lowered
and the (i) raised, not necessarily as far as (j). In (uw)
the consonant is more marked, and consequently is not
often made narrow, and the vowel seems to be as often
full (*u*) as not.

The three longs (æhɪ), (aɪ), and (ɔɪ), though not marked
as diphthongs, are not purely monophthongic, especially
the two back ones, which end with a raising of the front
of the tongue towards the mid-mixed position, although it
is not marked enough to be written. Indeed a full (ɔ[ʌ])
would have the effect of (o*i*h).

---

[a] The complicated scheme of unaccented vowels given by
Mr. Bell is peculiar to himself, and seems to be due solely to
artificial elocutionary habits.

The consonants are as follows :—

н		j	r	th, dh	s, z	sh, zh		wh, w	f, v
—					1		—	—	—
	k, g				t, d		p, b		
—	q				n		m		

(j) is often weakened into an (*i*h)-glide, but it is not easy to distinguish between them. (l), (t), (d), and (n) seem to be generally blade-consonants, corresponding to (s) and (z).

As regards the synthesis, E. consonants are joined together as much as possible without glides : there is no (æk[н]t) or (s*i*l[ʌ]k), &c.

The only B. R. consonant letters that differ from the N. R. ones are these :—

$$c = (\text{tṣh}) \quad as \ in \quad \textit{church.}$$
$$j = (\text{dẓh}) \quad ,, \quad \textit{judge.}$$
$$y = (j) \quad ,, \quad \textit{young.}$$
$$x = (\text{ks}) \quad ,, \quad \textit{six.}$$

The following specimens are intended to give as accurate a representation as I can of my own natural English pronunciation—the only one which I profess to have studied with any degree of exactness. I may note that my (wh) is an artificial sound for the natural (w) of South English. Otherwise my pronunciation is entirely natural and untaught—as much so as that of any savage[a].

No rules can be given for the pronunciation of those consonants that I have enclosed in parentheses in the

---

I never was taught either English pronunciation or English grammar at school.

B. R. notation, but I believe I always drop them in rapid speech, although they come out in slow reading.

It will be observed that all the pieces are divided by stress, or 'barred,' although in one of the B. R. ones the word-division is made by italics.

Pauses are occasionally indicated by (.).

A. Colloquial Phrases.

(Intended to bring out the separate elementary sounds.)

1. *In Narrow Romic.*

1. keme·pʌt ·wens \

2. : dhise¹zdhʌ thæhɪɪd tehɪhɪmeh·ɪhv ᵃ hæhɪdʌve¹zɪe¹ tæhɪɪn \

3. − hɪj ᵇ deznts·ɪɪjmtʌ (·)fɪɪjle¹tʌ (·)tɔɪl \ ᶜ

4. hɪɪʌrʌn ᵈ dhæɪʌrʌn ·evɪre¹wh·æɪʌ \

5. − dheɪh ·kerɪhm bækdhʌ ᵉ serɪhm deɪɪh \

6. − dhʌ mænɪuh·æddhʌ ·hæetɪʌnɪhz hedɪ \

7. kɔkɪne¹z semɪt·ehɪhɪmz ·ferɪhltʌdɪhs tɪqɪgwe¹shbʌ twɪɪjndhʌ ··hæɪɪrʌndheʌ hedɪzʌndhe¹ ··æɪɪʌwɪj brɪɪjdh \

8. − dhʌ ·boɪhɪ aɪs(k)te¹z faɪdhʌre¹fɪj wudntr·aɪdhʌ goo¹ʌl·ɪtl faɪdhʌ \

9. − behɪh ·ɔɪl mɪɪjnz sedɪe¹zpʌ paɪ \ − ehɪhm ·kwehɪht rede¹ \

10. : hæhʌw ·hehɪhɪe¹zdh·æt tæhʌwɪʌɪʌ bæhʌwt \

ᵃ In (ɪhɪ) the (ɪ) refers only to the length of the glide.

ᵇ Decidedly wide because unaccented.

ᶜ There may be an extra strong stress either on the last or the last but one group, according to the feeling of the speaker.

ᵈ Or (hɪjʌrʌn). The (ʌ) before the (r) in this and the next group is often very slight.

ᵉ Or (keihm ·bækɪ).

I

11. fıfte¹ʌw sıkste¹ fijtehıhshʌd thıqk \

12. whɔtʌ ·pıte¹jɯw lɔıste¹t \

13. – hıjwʌz ·pu/ıdæh·ʌwtʌ(v)dhʌ puıwlʌn pu/ıtʌ bedı \

14. – we¹l juwk·ɛm tuıw / – ehıh doo¹nt noıo¹ \

15. : djɯwʌb dzhek(t)tʌ(w)tʌ ᵃ ·bækʌws·moo¹k / –nɔtʌ
tɔıl \

16. – ehıh sɔıe¹m dzhıhstfʌrʌ moıo¹mıhntʌtdhʌ dɔııʌ\

17. – e¹ts hehıht·ehıhmdh·æt boıhıwʌ sent(t)ʌ ·skuıwl \
– hıyz tuwn·oıhıze¹ʌt hoıo¹m \

18. – hıj trehıhıdtʌ tijtshdhʌ tṣhehıhıld ·dẓhæhıımʌn \

19. : sevn sıksthsʌn ᵇ : tenʌ levnths \ ᶜ

20. whıṭshw·ɛn wɔze¹t \

21. – ehıh thɔıtdhʌt dhætıwʌz ɔııl ·dɛnıwe¹dh \

22. – jɯw dẓhɛdızhde¹mɛ·n dẓhɛstle¹ \–yɯwd·ıde¹n dııjd \

2. *The same in English Broad Romic.*

1. kəmə·pət ·wəns \

2. : dhisezdhə ·thəəd taima·iv həədəvezre təən \

3. – hiy dəznts·iymtə fiyletə taol \

4. hiiərən dhaerən ·evrewhaeə \

5. – dhei keim bækdhə seim dei \

6. – dhə mænuh·æddhə ·hætənez hed \

7. koknez səmt·aimz ·feiltədes tiqgweshbə twiyndhə
··haerəndheʌ hedzəndhe ··aeəwiy briydh \

8. – dhə boi aas(k)tez faadhərefiy wudntr·aadhə gouə
litl faadhə \

9. – bai ·aol miynz sedezpə paa \ – aim ·kwaıt rede \

ᵃ (dẓhekt . . .) or (dzhekı). The last syllable but one varies
between (uḅ), (ʌw), and (ʌ), according to the rapidity of pronunciation.

ᵇ Generally (sıksıʌn).

ᶜ Generally (levnsı).

10. – hau haiezdh·æt tauərə baut \

11. fifteo sixte ·fiytaishʌd thiqk \

12. whotə ·piteyuw laostet \

13. – hiywəz puldautə(v)dhə puwlən puttə bed \

14. – wel yuwk·əm tuw /. – ai dount nou \

15. : dyuwəb jekt(t)ətə bækos·mouk /. notə taol \

16. – ai saoem jestfərə moumentətdhə daoə \

17. – ets hait·aimdh·æt boiwə sent(t)ə ·skuwl \ – hiyz tuwn·oizeət houm \

18. – hiy traidtə tiycdhə caild ·jəəmən \

19. sevn sixthsən tenə levnths \

20. whicw·ən wozet \

21. – ai thaotdhət dhætwəz aol ·dənwedh \

22. – juw jəjdemə·n jəstle \ – yuwd·iden diyd \

B. PROSE.

(For comparison with the pronunciations given by Mr. Ellis, E. E. P., p. 1206.)

1. *In Narrow Romic.*

– dhʌ rítɪnʌn prɪnte¹dr·eprʌzʌn teɪhshʌnʌvdhʌ sæhʌwɪnz-ʌv læqɪgwe¹dʒh

– behɪh mɪɪjnzʌv kære¹ktʌzwh·ɪtṣhʌrí·nsʌ físhʌntb·oo¹th-e¹n kehɪhɪndʌn nɛmɪbʌ /

– ʌndwh·ɪtṣhmʌs(t) dhærʌfʌwb·ijkʌm behɪhɪndʌw məde¹ :fehɪhɪd /

: ífwɪjwudg·ívʌ græfe¹kʌls·imɪbʌlehɪh zeɪhshʌnʌvdhʌ :foo¹ nete¹k ele¹mʌnts

– we¹dh oɪo¹nle¹ ·sɛmɪde¹ griɪjʌve¹g zæktne¹sʌnkʌn ª viɪjnjʌns /

ª Also (zækɪn . . .).

– hʌz biɪjnfrʌm ˙ɔɪıl tehɪhɪm˙z /

– fʌ ˙neɪhshʌnzʌz welɪʌziˑnde¹ ˙vidẓhuʌl˙z /

: lɪqɪ gwɪste¹kʌl stjuıwdʌntsn˙ɔte¹k sepɪte¹d /
wɛnʌvdhʌm˙oo¹st ˙nese¹sre¹

– ʌnd wɛnʌvdhʌm˙oo¹st ˙dɪfe¹kʌltʌv prɔbɪle¹m˙z \

– ʌndʌz kɔnse¹kwʌntle¹ skæɑsle¹ ˙evʌbˑijn hæpe¹le¹
sɔlɪvd \

2. *In Broad Romic (with the word-division marked).*

– ₫hə ritnən printedr˙eprəzən teishənɔvdhə ꜱaun(d)zɔv
lɑqgwej

– ƀai miynzɔv ₭ærektɔzꜱhicɔrinˑsɔ fishʌntƀ˙outhen
₭aindən nɔmbɔ /

– ɔndꜱh icmɔst ₫haeɔfoƀiy₭əm baindɒ ꟽodefaid /

: iꜱwiywudg˙ivə græfekəlꜱ˙imbəlai zeishənɔvdhɔf˙ou netek
elemɔnts

– wedh ounle ˙ꜱɔmₔe griyɔveg zæk(t)nesənₖən viynyɔns /

–hɔz ƀiynfrəm ˙aol ꞇaimz /

–fə neishənzəz welɔziˑnde vijuɔlz /

: ₤iq gwistekɔl ꜱtyuwdʌntsꞥotek septed /
wɔnɔvdhɔm˙oust ˙nesesre

– ɔnd wɔnɔvdhɔm˙oust ˙ₔifekɔltɔv ꝓroblemz \

– ɔndɔz ₭onsekwɔntle ꜱkaeɔsle ˙evɔb˙iyn ꜧæpele ꜱolvd \

C. POETRY.

1. *In Narrow Romic.*

(This piece is given on account of its marked rhythm.)

– dhʌ kæpɪte¹vjuw zæhɪpʌ

: hæhɪıld dæhʌꜱinfrʌmdhʌ throıo¹n \

: leɪɪh bære¹de¹n tɔıpʌ /

– fʌ gətɪnʌnd loɪoˡnˏ

– eh*i*h brooˡktʊнeˡz slɛmɪbʌzˏ

– eh*i*h sh*i*vʌdнeˡz tṣher*i*hnˏ

– eh*i*h liɪgdнeˡmweˡdh nɛmɪbʌzˏ

– hijz ˙teh*i*h*i*rʌntʌ ger*i*hnˏ

: w*i*dhdhʌ blɛdɪʌvʌ m*i*l*i*jʌnнijl aɪnsʌmeh*i*h kæɪɪʌˏ

: w*i*dhʌ ne*i*hshʌ·nzdeˡ strɛkshʌnɪeˡz fl*e*h*i*htʌndeˡ spæɪɪʌˏ

2. *In Broad Romic.*

(Showing a variety of metres.)

(1)

– ənd sloule aansəd aathəfrəmdhə baajˏ.

– dhe ˙ould aodə ceinjethˏ   yiyldiq pleistə nyuwˏ

– ənd godful filzhim selfin ˙mene weizˏ

: lest ˙wən gud kəstəmsh·udkə rəptdhə wəəldˏ.

kəmfətdhai selfˏ.   : whot kəmfətizin ˙miyˏ.

– aiv ˙livdmai laifˏ   – ənd dhætwhicai·əv dən

: mei hiywidh in(h)im self meik pyuuəˏ   – bət dhau⁄

– if dhaushudst nevə siymai feisə genˏ

˙preifəmai soulˏ.   ˙maoə thiqzaa raotbai praeə

– dhəndh·is wəəld ˙driymz ovˏ.   whaeəfoə [a] letdhai vois

raizl·aikə fauntənfoəmi deiən(d) naitˏ.

– foə whotaa men betədhən shiypən(d) gouts⁄

– dhət nəreshə blaind laifwidh indhə brein⁄

– if nouiq goddhei liftnot hæn(d)zəv praeə

: bouthfədhəm selvzən(d) dhouzhu kaoldhəm frendˏ

– foə soudhə houl raund əəthiz evri wei

baundbai gould ccinzə bautdhə fiytəv godˏ.

– bət nauf·aeə welˏ.   – aim gouiqə loq wei

[a] = (. . . fɔʌ) or (. . . fʌw).

– widh dhiyz dhau siyest⟋   – ifin diydai gou⟋
– fər aolmai maindez klaudedwidhə daut⟋
– tudhe ailənd væleəv ˙æviljon ᵃ ⟍
: whaeə faolznot ḣeiloə reinor eni snou ⟍
– nor evə wind blouz laudle ⟍   – bətet laiz
diypm˙edoud hæpe faeəwidh aocəəd laonz ⟍
– ən(d) bauəre holouz kraundwidh səmə siy ⟍
: whaerai˙wil hiylmiyəvmai griyvəs wuwnd ⟍.
– sou sed(h)ij ⟍   – ən(d)dhe baajwidh aorən seil
muwvdfrəmdhə briqkl˙aiks˙əm fulb˙rested swon⟋
– dhət fluwtiqə waild kærəl aeəhəə deth⟋
rəflzhəə pyuuə kould pluwmzən teixdhə fləd
– widh swaothe webz ⟍. loq studsəə bedeviiə
– re volviq mene memərez⟋   – tildhə həl
lukt wən blæk dotə genstdhə vəəjəv daon ⟍
– əndo˙ndhə miiədhə weiliq daidə wei ⟍

(2)

swiftle waok ouvədhə westəən weiv
                    spiritəv nait ⟍
autəvdhə miste iystəən keiv⟋
whaer aoldhə loqən(d) loun dei lait
– dhau wouvest driymzəv joiən fiiə⟋
– whic meikdhiy terebələn diiə ⟍
                    swiftbiydhai flait ⟍

ræpdhai faominə mæntl grei ⟍
                    staari˙n raot ⟍
blaindwidhdhain haeədhe aizəv dei ⟍
kis(h)ərən tilshiybiy wiiəred aut
: dhen wondəraoə siteən siyən lænd⟋

ᵃ Or ‘ æviljən ’.

təciq aolwidhdhain oupyeit[a] wond
        kəm loq saot

: whenai rouzən saodhə daon /
– when lait roud haiəndhə dyuwwəz gaon[b] /
– ənd nuwn lei heveon flauərərən triy /
– ənddhə wiiəre dei təəndtu(h)iz rest /
liqgəriq laikən ənl·əvd gest /
        ai ·saidfə dhiy \

– dhai brədhə deth keimən kraid /
        wudstdhau miy /
– dhai swiyt caild sliypdhə filmeai·d
məəməd laikə nuwnt·aid biy /
shælai nesl niiədhai said /
wudstdhau miy / – əndaire plaid \
        nou — not dhiy \

dethwil kəmwhen dhauaat ded \
        suwn tuw suwn \
sliypwil kəmwhen dhauaat fled \
– əv naidhə [c]wudai aaskdhə buwn \
– ai aaskəv dhiybe ləved nait
swiftbiy dhainə prouciq flait \
        kəm suwn suwn \

(3)

inə driiən·aitedde sembə –
tuw ·hæpe ·hæpe triy \
– dhai braanshez naeəre membə
– dheə griynfe lisete \

---

[a] Or 'oupyet'.   [b] Or 'gon'.   [c] Or 'nüdhə'.

– dhə naothkən notə·n duwdhəm
widhə sliyte whisl thruwdhəm \
– noə frouzn thaoiqz gluwdhəm
– frəm bədiqətdhə praim \

inə driiən·aitedde sembə –
tuw ·hæpe ·hæpe bruk \
– dhai bəbliqz naeəre membə
– ə polouz səmə luk \
– bət widhə swiytfə getiq
– dhei steidheə kristəl fretiq \
nevə nevə petiq
– ə bautdhə frouzn taim \

aa wudt·wəə souwidh mene
– ə jentl gəələn boi \
– bət wəədhər evər ene
raidhdnotət paased joi /
– tə noudhə ceinjən fiylit \
: whendhəriz nəntə hiylit \
– noə nəmed senstə stiylit \
– wəz nevə sedin raim \

(4)

: huw ruwindmiyaerai·wəz baon \
sould evre eikə graasoə kaon \
– ənd leftdhə next aer aolfə laon \
    – mai ·grænf·aadhə \

: huw sedmai mədhəwoz·nou nəəs
– ənd fisektmiyən meidmiy wəəs
– til infənsebe keimə kəəs
    – mai ·grænm·ədhə

: huw leftmiyi·nmai sevnth yiiə
— ə kəmfətəmai mədhə diiə
— ənd mistə poupdhe ouvəs·iiə
    — mai ·faadhə

: huw letmiy staavtə baiəə jin
— til aolmai bounz keim thruwmai skin
dhen kaoldmiy əgle litl sin
    — mai ·mədhə

: huwəv aol əəthle thiqzw·ud boust
— hiy heited ədhəz brætsdhə moust
— ən dhaeəfo [a] meidmiy fiylmai poust
    — mai ·əqkl

: huw goten skreipsən endles skaoə
— ənd aolwez leiddhəmətmai daoə
— til meneə bitə bæqai baoə
    — mai ·kəzn

: huw tukmiy houmwhen mədhə daid
— ə genwidh faadhətərezaid
blæk shuwz kliyn naivz rən faarən waid
    — mai ·stepm·ədhə

: huw maadmai stelthe əəcenjoiz
— ənd whenai pleid kraid ·whotə noiz
gəəlz aolwez hektər ouvə boiz
    — mai ·sistə

:huw yuws(t)tə shaeren whotwəz main
— aoə tukit ·aoldidh·iyen klain
koz aiwəz eitən hiywəz nain
    — mai ·brədhə

[a] = (ʌw).

:huw strouktmai hed – ən sed gud læd\
– ən geivmiy sixpəns\ aol(h)iy hæd ⁄
:bətətdhə staoldhə koinwəz bæd ⁄
            – mai ·godf·aadhə\

:huw greites shaeədmai soushəl glaas
– bət whenm·is faocən keimtə paas
– re fəədmiytədhə pəmp – ə laas
            – mai ·frend

– thruw aoldhis wiiəre wəəlden briyf
huw evə simpəthaizden griyf
– oə shaeədmai joi – mai soulre liyf
            mai ·self\

FRENCH.

		i			
	eh	e	a		e
	æhq	æ,æq	aq		
u		y			
o		ə	o,oq	oh	ə
		œ			

Observe the simplicity of the vowel-system, the fewness
of wide vowels, the absence of unrounded back-narrow
vowels, and the full development of the front-round
vowels; the absence of diphthongs (which are represented by consonant-combinations), and the peculiar
gutturo-nasal vowels (to which we will return hereafter)
—everything directly opposed to English.

(e) is often raised towards (i), and its narrowness, like

that of all the other vowels, is very marked. (i) and (u) are often very high, amounting almost to consonants, (j) and (w). (æ) and (œ) are often very low, and are generally long at the same time, but there are various intermediate degrees of lowering which seem to be unfixed and arbitrary. When raised towards the mid-position, it is not easy to distinguish them from (*e*) and (*ə*), which French grammarians call 'moyen-ouvert.' (eh) is not the same sound as in the Teutonic languages [a]: it seems to be the outer sound (ęh), and appears to interchange with (ə), which it closely resembles.

(a) generally tends towards (ạ), whether written *a* or *â*, but is sometimes full (a) when long. (o) and (*o*) are generally advanced towards the mixed position, and this is especially noticeable with short (*o*), which often seems to be regular (oh).

The nasal vowels vary greatly:—

æhɋ, ehɋ, œhɋ, ɐɋ (Bell).
aɋ, aɋ, ɔhɋ (Bell).
æɋ, æɋ
oɋ, ohɋ (Bell).

The correspondence of the French Broad Romic letters is as follows :—

a	=	(a)	*as in*	chat.
aq	=	(*a*ɋ)	„	dent.
æ	=	(æ), (*e*)	„	père, dette.
æq	=	(æɋ)	„	vin.
e	=	(e)	„	été.

[a] Professor Storm, of Christiania, one of the most acute of living phoneticians, told me that the French (eh) is distinct from the Norwegian unaccented *e*, which he identifies with the German.

ə = (eh)   *as in*   que.

əə[a] = (ə)   ,,   p*eu*.

əq = (æhq)   ,,   *un*.

i = (i)   ,,   f*i*n*i*.

o = (o)   ,,   be*au*.

oq = (*o*q)   ,,   s*o*n.

ɔ = (*o*), (*o*h)   ,,   *or*, d*o*tte.

œ = (œ), (ə)   ,,   v*eu*f, v*eu*vage.

y = (y)   ,,   l*u*ne.

The consonants are :—

		jh,j	rh*r*,r*r*		s,z	sh,zh		wh,w	f,v
—			lh,ḷ						
	k,g		ṭ,ḍ				p,b		
—		N	ṇ				m		

(phj) and (bhj) also occur.

Note the absence of (H)[b] and (q). Otherwise there is a certain similarity between the French and English system, both rejecting (kh) and developing fully the blade consonants.

All the consonants are narrow, which is especially noticeable in (w) and (bhj). The point and blade open consonants (r, s, sh, &c.) are more forward than the English ones. For (rr) (ghr) is often substituted. (N) sometimes seems to become (jn).

[a] Written double to distinguish it from ə = (eh), which is never fully long. Full long (ə) must be written əəə, if necessary; but the marking of quantity is practically unimportant.

This sound is, however, often formed involuntarily by Frenchmen. I have heard it in the exclamation (hoɪ) for (oɪ), in (fleho) for (fleo) = *fléau*, &c.

Consonant-glides are more noticeable in French than in English, especially in stop-combinations, (strik[ʜ]t)= 'strict.' Final voice stops often end in a voice-glide, (bag[ʌ])='bague.' In passing from (ɴ) to the next vowel the glide is generally formed so slowly as to be heard as a separate element, so that (ohɴ[i]oq)='oignon' sounds like (ohɴjoq). Final (j) and (ɴ)[a] end voicelessly, the glottis being opened at the moment of removing the tongue from the consonant position, so that (fijʜ) and (viɴʜ) sound like (fij-jh) and (viɴ-jh).

In Broad Romic *ph*=(phj), *bh*=(bhj), *nh*=(ɴ).

The quantity of the vowels[b] is very uncertain. The only constantly short vowel is (eh), although even it is sometimes lengthened in such words as *peser* (pehze). Final vowels when accented are also often short, as in *oui* (wi). Full long vowels are commonest before (rr), and then before the hiss and buzz open consonants, as in *faire* (fæɪrr), *rage* (raɪzh). Nasal vowels are short when final and accented, full long before consonants: compare *son* (soq) with *songe* (soqɪzh). Exclamations, such as *ah* (aɪ), *oh* (oɪ), are generally long. The distinctions of quantity are most marked in final syllables. Medially all vowels tend to half-long quantity. Compare *France* (frraqɪs) with *Français* (frraqsæ), the first with long, the second with half-long (aq). In all other cases vowels vary between short and half-long, as in E. vowels before voiceless consonants. In rapid speech the distinctions of quantity become still more vague. In writing French it is best to leave the medium quantity unmarked, denoting shortness by (˘) after the vowel and full length by (ɪ).

[a] Not (l).   [b] Consonants are short.

The force of the separate syllables is nearly equal throughout, and the consonants are always uttered with the same strong force. Thus in *été* the force is nearly equal throughout, and the (t) is pronounced with the same force as in the E. 'teacup,' and there is none of that rapid diminution and sudden increase of force that characterises the E. 'take up.' Hence to an English ear *été* appears to be divided (e·-t·e), although Englishmen speaking French generally make it into (e·ïht-eïh). There is, in fact, no syllabification in French, and, as the same principles are carried out in sentences as well, there is no word-division. Thus *un grand homme* suggests (æhq g·rraqı t·ohm).

The word-stress is generally on the first syllable [a]. The exceptions are words in *a* followed by a consonant or consonants and then by *ion*, which always take the stress on the *a*, as in *occasion* (ohk·aizjoq). When the vowel is not *a* the stress varies. Exceptions occur also in other words of several syllables, and there is altogether much uncertainty and variation.

Sentence-stress is very irregular. There is no such thing as logical emphasis, no marking of antithesis, as in the E. 'to *give* and *for*give,' 'not *you*, but *he.*' French sentence-stress is mainly emotional, not logical. Words with which any strong feeling is associated are naturally pronounced with force in French as in other languages, but French has made a peculiar extension of this emotional principle, which consists first in accenting *intensitive*

---

[a] This view of French accentuation was first advanced by Rapp, in his 'Physiologie der Sprache,' so far back as 1840, and again by a Frenchman, Professor C. Cassal, in the Transactions of the Philological Society, 1873-4. It is, however, not admitted by the majority of French philologists.

words such as *très*, as in ' très-bien,' '*guère*,' '*quel* sup-
plice !' &c.; and then in accenting modifying words
generally, such as the negative *pas*, &c., as in ' il n'est
pas ici.' But there is great laxity and arbitrariness
generally, which makes it difficult for Frenchmen to discriminate force either in their own or in foreign languages.

Stress and quantity are independent in French. Thus
in *bavard* (bavaɪrr) and *finir* (finiɪrr), the first vowel in
each word is half-long and accented (strong), the second
full-long and unaccented, or rather half-strong. (eh) is,
however, almost always both fully short and weak-stressed.
There is also a certain rhythmic tendency both in stress
and quantity, although it is not well defined, which leads
to the alternation of strong and weak stress, long and
short quantity in various degrees.

Tone is very rudimentary. Although question and
doubt is generally expressed by a rise, French intonation
is otherwise more emotional than logical. The tone in
French generally runs straight on in one direction, and
appears to be more level than in E. The rising tone is
often used in simple statements.

Altogether French is characterised by the almost complete absence of synthesis distinctions, and the existing
distinctions may be disregarded without materially affect-
ing the intelligibility of the context. These wants are,
however, fully compensated by the clear, energetic articulation of the consonants, the purity of the vowels, and the
sonorousness of the nasal vowels. No language combines
power and harmony with elegance and brevity more successfully than French.

In the following specimens the marks of quantity
and stress must be taken to represent in many cases

possibilities only, not necessities, nor are they introduced
uniformly throughout.   The sentences are divided into as
short groups as possible without any reference to stress,
which is marked by (˙) in the body of the groups.   The
unmarked syllables must be understood to be uttered with
medium force, but the mark of medium force (:) has been
occasionally introduced especially to call attention to cases
of equal stress, and as a reminder in other cases.   It must
be remembered that (eh) is generally quite short and weak-
stressed, except when specially marked.

A. Sentences.

k˙eh˙vulevu.   keskseksa˙.   1
ilfoto˙p˙arra˙vaq˙ kehzhrrehturrna˙parri˙.
zhehv:walarrka˙qsjel.
kelaɪ˙zhave˙vu˙.   ila˙væqɪtaq˙paɪse˙.   ilelene.
kæɪs.   zhn˙erriæq.   kelœɪrræɪ˙s.   ilet˙aɪrr.   5
de˙peshe˙vudvuzabi˙je˙.   ilparrldyne.
soqpubafoɪrr.   zhehvufrret˙uvwaɪrr.
us˙ohmnu˙mæqɪtaq.
vuvuziprrehnef˙o˙ɪrrgoshmaq.
ilnek˙ynœɪrr.   zheydybohnœɪrr.   10
lehtaqɪze˙klæɪrr.   lehtaqsehrrmetobo.
ilaq˙maqɪkæhq˙.   ohna˙parrledlaplbhɟiedybotaq.
oqniv˙wagut.   setaɪq˙nbhɟi˙jə.   zhanease˙
vwalabhɟ˙izhuɪrr kehzhehnsbhɟisorrti˙.
lwazivteelamæɪrrdeht˙ulevis.   15
lehsohlæɪjsehlæɪv.   illbhɟiarraqɪdylaparræijн.
prretemwaynfœjdpapjhe.   setæhqboku˙˙dœijн.
nu˙nusohmlie˙damitjhe˙   forrte˙trrwatmaq˙.
pur˙rkwhanparr˙levup:a˙.   k˙eh˙pphɟizhf˙æɪrrpurrvu˙.
k˙eskkilaqsænн.   ilaqseɴlehlatæq.   zhehmvebeɴ[i]e.   20

zhehvjæɋdyteaɪtrh*r*. lehtwhaɪlsehlæɪv.

sezha*ɋ*nehso*ɋ*pavnyzospek(н)taɪklh pur*r*vuza*ɋt·*a*ɋ*ɪdrh*r*ᵃ.

English Translation.

: who(t)dəyuw wont \.   : whot izet \.

: aiməst fəəstre təəntə pæres \.

– ai siydhə reinb·ou \.

– hau ouldayuw \.   : hiyez ouvə ·twente \.   – hiyzdhe
ouldest \.

: whot ·izet \ (: whotsdhə mætə \). nətheq \. whotsdhə
taim \.   – ets leit \.   5

: meik heistən dres \.   – hiy spiyxthruwez nouz \.

– hez pəls biyts faast \.   – ail shouyuw ·evrethiq \.

– whaer aawin·au \.

– yuw gouə bautet vere aokwədle \.

– ets ounlᶒ ·wən \.   – aivh·æd lək \.   10

– dhə wedhəz kliiə \.   – dhə wedhəzem pruwveq \.

– dhəəz ·wən miseq \.   – dhei taoktəvdhə reinən fain
wedhə \.

– yuw kaants iiə taol \.   – ets taiəsəm \.   – aiv hæde
nəfəvet \.

– ets nau ·eit deizsi·nsaivbiyn eibltəg·ou aut \.

aidlnezezdhə mədhərəv aol vaisez \.   15

– dhə ·sən raizez \.   – hiəz peidem bækendhə seim
koin \.

ᵃ This is an instructive instance of what would be entirely false
emphasis in any language but French. The sense is, of course,
'they have not come to hear *you*, but the play,' but French accent
suggests to an English ear, 'they have not come to *hear* you (but to
see you '). There is no necessity for accenting (a*ɋ*ta*ɋ*ɪdrh*r*) any more
than (vuz)—the essential point to be observed is the *meaninglessness*
of the accent.

K

lendmiə shiytəv peipə \.   – itsə ˙fain vjuw \

– wiə verɛ intəmetle baunden frenshep \

: whaidountyuw spiyk \.   : whotkənai duwfəyuw \.

: who(t)dəzij tiyc \. – hiy tiycez læten \. – aim goueqtə

˙beidh \   20

  – ai kəmfrəmdhə thiiətə \.   – dhə kəətn raizez \.

: dhiyz piypləv not kəmtədhə thiiətətə hiiə ˙yuw \

B. Prose.

  – leh˙m:arʀki˙netæpurʀtaq˙ p˙azæhnohmdehzheni˙ \
iletæsavaq˙ / – mæs:avaq˙saq˙spesi˙alite˙ \
amwaqkoqɪnvœja˙plerʀæqɪsi /
yng˙rraqɪda˙bili˙te pursærʀtæqɪzuvrʀaɪzh s˙aqɪzy˙tili˙te
okyn /
doqnuzorroqɪzase˙suvaq˙ljədparʀleplyt˙aɪrr /
e˙ki˙avæta˙psorʀbe   zhyska˙la˙paɪsjoq   zhyska˙la˙
m˙ohnoh˙mani˙ /
led idærʀnjæɪrrzanedsohnegzistaqɪs \
shoze˙t˙rraqɪzh /
e˙ki˙netæp˙azæhqdekohtelem˙waqmisterrjə dehsoh˙norʀ-
ga˙ni˙z˙aɪsjoqudsoh˙ny˙mœɪrr /
malgrʀelorʀgœijdsoqn˙oq edsaf orrtyn /
ilnavæzhamæsoqɪzheasmarrje \
rrehmetaqtuzhuɪrrzolaqɪdmæq sehd˙erraqɪzhmaqdaqsez-
a˙bi˙tyd \
apsorʀbe˙parʀdeze˙tyd taqɪtoserrjəɪz taqɪtofrrivol /
e˙doh˙naqprʀeskehtuzhuɪrrlaprʀe˙ſe˙rraqɪsa˙selsi˙ /
ilavæs˙i˙biæqkoqɪplike saviæqɪterʀjœɪrr /
illavætohpstrrye deht aqdehp˙rrohzhe dehf aqɪtezi
dehkyrri˙ozi˙tez edehspeky˙laɪsjoqɪzæqɪtelek[н]tyæl /

kilnavæzh·amæ‑trɾuve‑ltɑqdetrɾərɾə /
eaɑɪkorɾmwɑq sehlbhʲi‑detrɾæhɑsavaɑfekoq \ ᵃ

C. POETRY (*in French Broad Romic*).

kaptiforivaazhdymaor
əqgærjekurbesusæfaer
dizæ \ zhəvurwazaqkaor
wazozænmidæzivaer
iroqdæl kɔlæsperaaqs
sbhizhyskaqsæbrylaqklima \
saqdutvukitelafraaqs \
dəmoqpæjnəməparlevupa /
dəpphitrwazaqzhəvukoqzhyyr
dəmaportæɾəqsuvniir
dyvaloq umaviopskyyr
səbæɾsædəqduzavniir \
odetuurdynokishmin
aflopyyrsudəfrælila
vuzavevynotrshomin \
dəsvaloqnəməparlevupa /

GERMAN.

The pronunciation here given is that of Hanover, the
only one of which I have enough knowledge. It is

The ordinary spelling of the first paragraph is as follows: Le
marquis n etait pourtant pas un homme de genie. Il etait savant,
mais savant sans specialite, a moins qu on ne veuille appeler ainsi
une grande habilité pour certains ouvrages sans utilité aucune, dont
nous aurons assez souvent lieu de parler plus tard, et qui avaient
absorbe jusqu'a la passion, jusqu a la monomanie, les dix dernières
annees de son existence.

virtually Middle-German as pronounced by a Low-German population.

		iɪ				*i*
	eh	eɪ	a(ɪ)			*e*
uɪ		yɪ	*u*			*y*
oɪ			*o*			ǝ(ɪ)

Diphthongs: (a*e*), (a*o*), (*oe*).

Observe the simplicity of the system and the fewness and distinctness of its diphthongs. Also the absence of low vowels. The only analogy with English is the widening of the short vowels. Wide vowels, except (a), cannot occur finally, but are made narrow, as in the proper names *Lili* (lïli), *Otto* (oto). Short narrow vowels occur also occasionally as the result of shortening.

(*i*) and (*u*) are not lowered, as in English, towards the mid-positions, and consequently have a closer sound. (a), especially when long, tends towards (a̜). The backround vowels are fully retracted, which gives them a deep sound. The front-rounds are also slightly retracted towards the mid-position, which deepens their tone.

In the schools an artificial distinction seems to be made between long *ä* and *e*, the first being pronounced (*e*ɪ), the second (eɪ).

In the diphthongs both elements are short under all circumstances. The second elements of the diphthongs are uncertain   The real sounds may be (*i*h) or *e*[1] and (ʌw) as in English. Certainly such a pronunciation as (ae¹), (aʌw), (oe¹) would not be detected as foreign The vowel-like consonants often generate a voice-glide before them, but only in final syllables, forming diphthongs which come out most clearly with high vowels. Compare *viel* (fiɪ[ʌ]l) with *viele* (fiɪleh).

The Broad Romic letters are :—

a	=	(a)	*as in*	m*a*nn
aa	=	(aɪ)	„	m*ah*nen
ai	=	(ae)	„	we*i*n
au	=	(ao)	„	ha*u*s.
e	=	(e)	„	mensch.
ee	=	(eɪ)	„	s*ee*.
ə	=	(eh), (ə)	„	end*e*, götter.
əə	=	(əɪ)	„	sch*ö*n.
i	=	(i)	„	b*i*n.
ii	=	(iɪ)	„	b*ie*ne.
o	=	(o)	„	sonne.
oo	=	(oɪ)	„	s*oh*n.
oi	=	(oe)	„	ne*u*.
u	=	(u)	„	*u*nd.
uu	=	(uɪ)	„	g*u*t.
y	=	(y)	„	sch*ü*tzen.
yy	=	(yɪ)	„	gr*ü*n.

The consonants are :—

R,H	kh,gh	jh,j			s,z	sh*w*			f,v
		l							
	k,g		t,d					p,b	
	q		n					m	

Final stops are always voiceless, and voiced buzzes (gh, j) becomes whispered ('gh, 'j), with perhaps some initial vocality. The voiceless stops at the beginning of a syllable (or word) are pronounced with greater force and expenditure of breath than in English. (gh) and (j) are always either buzzed or strongly squeezed. The front consonants seem to be generally (ˌjh) and (ˌj). The point consonants are more forward than the English, and seem as in the other Teutonic languages, to be formed on the teeth-rim—they are therefore ' half-dental.'

(ʀ) is really [ʀæh], the tongue being in the low-mixed position while the super-glottal contraction takes place, which is not very strong. (ghr) is also heard, especially on the stage[1] (khw) occurs after (u) and (ao), as in *auch* (aokhw). (l) is ' higher' (more palatal) than in English, though not so much so as in French. Initial (z) is (sʌ). (zh) occurs in French words, but is a purely artificial sound. (p) in the combination (pf) is often the teeth-lip instead of the simple lip stop. (v) is not strongly buzzed as in English and French, and is often formed so weak as very much to resemble (bh).

Stops are oftener joined by glides than in English, and in such combinations as initial (kn) in *knie* there is often a distinct breath-glide between the (k) and the (n)— (k[ʜ]niɪ).

The special Broad Romic consonant letters are the following :—

x	=	(kh), (khw)	*as in*	nac*h*, auc*h*.
gh	=	('gh)	,,	la*g*.

I once heard a strong (rr) in Hildesheim from an apparent native.

j	=	(j)	*as in*	*j*a.
r	=	(ʀ)	,,	*r*etter.
c	=	(jh)	,,	i*ch*.

(w) is reserved for the M. and S. G. (bh) = N. G. (v).

In the quantity it must be noted that long vowels are not shortened before voiceless consonants, as in English, the vowel in *noth* (noɪt), for instance, being as long as in the E. *node*, not half-long as in *note*. The short vowels seem, on the other hand, to be shorter than the English : compare *bitter* (bɪtehʀ) with the E. (bɪtʌ). Final consonants are always short: compare *mann* (man) with the E. *man* = (mænɪ) or (mæɪn). Vowel-like consonants are, however, lengthened before voiced stops as in E. Compare *bilden* (bɪlɪdehn) with *halten* (haltehn).

Force (stress) and intonation are very similar in the two languages.

In the following specimens (.) is put before voiceless stops when they are pronounced strongly. The quantity is marked by (ɪ) only, but it must be understood that in all syllables which have not the full accent the long vowels are somewhat shortened.

A. Sentences.

– vas haɪbmz*i*da \ [a]. s[ʌ]aɪgehnz*i*maɪl \   – vi haest – diizeh stʀaɪseh \.

– vi fiɪʌl volnz*i* m*i*tn·eɪmehn \. : s[ʌ]*i*nts[ʌ]*i* feʀt*i̇*j /.

– maen heʀ / – s[ʌ]i *i*ʀns[ʌ]*i*jh gansʊn(t) gaɪʀ \.

: vi laq*i*s(t)dehʀ veɪ j \.

Also (haɪbmzeh . . .) or even (haɪmɪzeh . . .). In these intimate combinations the (z) seems to be fully vocal, not = (s[ʌ]).

– ijh s[ʌ]uɪkhwehdas buɪkhw ꜟ. moʀgehns tʋnɪdehhat
golɪtimmʋnɪdeh ꜟ.
 – vo voɪntehʀ ꜟ.   – eʀ voɪnt tsvae tʀepm hoɪkh ꜟ
– ijh məjhtehtsʋ ʀyk k eɪʀehn ꜟ.   gʀyɪsnzüɪnfon miɪʀ ꜟ
həɪʀehnzehmˑaɪl ꜟ daɪ.kˑəntijhiɪˑnɪn shwəɪnehgeh shwijh-
tehfonehʀ tseɪln ꜟ
  – eʀ giqaˑosdehm ᵃ haozeh ꜟ
 : eʀɥat tsvae noeeh hoezehʀgeh .kaoft ꜟ

English Translation.

 : whotəvyuw gotdhaeə ꜟ.   – wilyuw telmiydhə neiməv-
dhis striyt ⁄
 – hau məcwilyuw teik widhyuw ꜟ.   : aayuw rede ⁄
səə ⁄ yuweh kwaitmes teikn ꜟ
 – hau loqezdhə wei ꜟ
 – aim lukeqfədhə buk ꜟ.   – dhə maoneq auəhəz gould
enets mauth ꜟ
 : whaeədəziy liv ꜟ.   – hiy livzondhə sekənd staore ꜟ
 : aishəd laiktətˑəən bæk ꜟ.   grɪytɥimfrəmmˑiy ꜟ
luk hiiə ꜟ   : aikəd telyuwə ˑprite staoreə bautet ꜟ
 – hiy wentaˑutəvdhə haus ꜟ
 – hiyəz baot tuw nyuw hauzez ꜟ

B. Prose.

faɪtehʀlˑendishweh   alteh   s[ʌ]aɪgehn ꜟ   : viɪehsmiɪr
shwaent ꜟ
 : haɪbmiɪˑʀehn ʀaetsɪnaˑenehʀgeh visn maqlɥˑaftɪ jkaet ꜟ
 : jaɪdehʀ glaobehbeh ʀuɪtmˑitda ʀaof ⁄
 : vaeldasgeh fyɪ[ʌ]laˑenehm s[ʌ]aɪˑght ⁄
 – dasdi lyɪgeh alehs aosspɪnɪn məjhteh ꜟ.

ᵃ Also (aosm).

: ᴜns[ʌ]ehʀeh eɪdlstehn veʀkehdɐs dʀaet·seɪntnj aɪʀ hᴜn-
dehʀts ⸗

— s[ʌ]ɪnt vɪ̇ʀkli̇ᵉjhs[ʌ]o tsaɪʀtgeh di̇jhtehtᴜnt aosgeh
:ʃyɪʀt \

: dass[ʌ]i̇jhdigeh ·shwi̇ktehsteh hanɪta·enehs noeehn
di̇jhtehʀsda ʀi̇nfehʀ gʀaɐfehnv·yɪʀdeh \.

— dehna·ɪʀi ostᴜnt taso .konti̇jh niɪmaɪlstsᴜ enɪdeh
leɪzn \

: vaɐlmiʀ foɪʀk·aɪm ⸗ — bae alehm glansehiɪʀehʀ voʀ-
tnᴜntem pfi̇nɪdᴜqehn ⸗ : s[ʌ]aedokhdina .tuɪʀdehʀ altn
folksd·ijhtᴜqi̇nir·nntsᴜ gʀᴜnɪtgeh gaqehn \.

: jeɪdeht·sᴜ gʀoɪseh fyleh lɐst wiɪdehʀ leɪʀ \.

— di ʀejhtehp oe ᵃ s[ʌ]iɪ ᵇ glaejhta·enehm menshwn ⸗

: deɪʀs[ʌ]i̇jh .taozntf elti̇ᵉjehʀ fʀoeehn.k·an ⸗

: voɪeʀ laopᴜnt gʀaɪs vaksn ⸗

— di s[ʌ]oneh aofᴜnt niɪdehʀg·eɪehn s[ʌ]iɪt \

— di ·falshweh aenehm deɪʀi̇n fʀemɪdeh lenɪdehʀ feɪʀt \

— ᴜnts·[ʌ]i̇jhandn beʀgqdehʀ shwvaets ⸗

— dehm hi̇mɪlᴜnt meɪʀi ·taɪljehnstsᴜehʀ heɪbm veɪnt \.
steɪtehʀnuɪ[ʌ]n mi̇tnda ʀi̇n ⸗

— s[ʌ]ov·i̇ʀts[ʌ]aenfehʀ gnyɪgqf·iɪ[ʌ]l laejht ·laqehni̇jht
ʀaejhehnandas maɪsdɐsda haemgehb·liɪbnehn \

: deɪms[ʌ]aen apflb aomi̇m haosg·aʀtn jeɪʀli̇jh blyɪt ⸗

— ᴜntdi fi̇qkqda ʀaof shwlaɪgq \

C. POETRY (*in Broad Romic*).

(1)

: oo zeestdu folər moondnsh·ain
— tsum ·letstn maalaufm·ainə pain \

(oe) in two syllables.   ᵇ Half-long.

: deenr·czo mancə mitərnaxt
– and·iizəm pulther angəw·axt \
dannyy·bər byycərnuntpa piir /
: tryyp zeeljhər ᵃ frointer shiinstd uum iir \
ax kənticd oxauf ·bergəsʜəən
– ind ainəm liibən lictə geeən \
– um bergəsh·əələmit gaistərn shveebən \
– auf ·viiznind·ainəm demər veebən \
– fon aləm visnsk valment laadn
– in dainəm taugə zuntmic baadn \

(2)

:yybər alən gipfəln
– ist ruu \
– in alən ꞏvipfəln
spyyrəstd·uu
kaumai·nən haux \
– di fəəgəlain shvaigənim valdə \
vartən·uur \ balde
ruuəst duu aux \

(3)

: duu bistviai·nə ·bluumə
: zoo ·holtunt ·shəənunt ·rain \
– ic shaudic an –unt ·veem·unt
shlaictmiirins hertsʜin ain \

– miiri·stalsopi·cdi hendə
– aufs hauptd·iir leegən zolt \
beetəntdas gotdicer haltə
: zoo ·rainunt ·shəənunt ·holt \.

ᵃ *jh* = (·j).

DUTCH[a].

		i(ɪ)			e¹
	eh	eɪ	ɑ̨ɪ		eɪ
	æh(i)	æ	a		
u(ɪ)		y(ɪ)			
o(ɪ)		əɪ	o(ɪ)		əɪ
		œ	ɔ		

The diphthongs are : aɪi, æhi, æhə, iu, eɪu, æi, ui, oɪi, ɔu, yu.

Both elements are short, except where the first is marked long. The second element (the glide-vowel) seems to be always narrow, as also in the diphthongised long vowels described below.

(e¹) is, perhaps, also (e¹). (a) varies : sometimes it is raised to (a), sometimes narrowed to (ɒ). The lowering of (æ) is very marked, and it sometimes passes into (æ). (œ) is often (ə) and (eh).

(eɪ), (oɪ), and (əɪ) are in some pronunciations diphthongised into (eɪi), (oɪu), and (əɪy), but not before (rr). Those who do not diphthongise these vowels widen them

---

[a] Compare Donders, De Physiologie der Spraakklanken, and Land, Over Uitspraak en Spelling. My knowledge of Dutch pronunciation was mainly acquired from personal hearing of Messrs. Donders, Land, and Kern. The only point in which I differ from them is in not considering (l) &c. in *bindloon*, &c. to be voiceless. It seems to me that the glide from the *d* (= t) to the (l) is all that is voiceless.

before (rr). We thus get the two following parallel pronunciations [a]:—

		(1)	(2)
steen	=	steɪin	steɪn.
meer	=	meɪɪr	meɪɪr.
boom	=	boɪum	boɪm.
door	=	doɪɪr	doɪɪr.
neus	=	nəɪys	nəɪs.
deur	=	dəɪɪr	dəɪɪr.

Short open *o*, as in 'slot,' is sometimes (o), sometimes
(ɔ); short close *o*, as in 'op,' is generally (o), often with a
peculiar guttural effect.

The following are the Broad Romic letters :—

			as in	
a	=	(a)	„	m*a*n.
aa	=	(aɪ)	„	m*aa*n.
aai	=	(aɪi)	„	fr*aai*.
e	=	(æ)	„	b*e*d.
ee	=	(eɪ), (eɪ), (eɪi)	„	st*ee*n, b*e*ter, m*ee*r.
eeu	=	(eɪu)	„	l*eeu*w.
ei	=	(æi)	„	r*ei*s, t*ij*d.
ə	=	(œ), (eh)	„	d*u*n, vad*e*r.
əə	=	(əɪ), (əɪ), əɪy	„	n*eu*s, d*eu*r.
əi	=	(æhi)	„	l*ui*.
əu	=	(æhə)	„	h*ui*s.
i	=	(i)	„	n*ie*t.
ii	=	(iɪ)	„	b*ie*r.
ie	=	(e¹)	„	v*i*sch.
iu	=	(iu)	„	n*ieu*w.

[a] The first is that of Professor Donders, the second of Professor
Land. The first seems to be the usual one in the province of
Holland.

o | = | (o) | | *as in* | *op.*
oo | = | (oɪ), (oɪ), (oɪu) | | ,, | b*oo*m, b*o*ven, d*oo*r.
ooi | = | (oɪi) | | ,, | m*ooi*.
ou | = | (ɒu), (ɔu) | | ,, | bla*auw*, k*ou*d.
ɔ | = | (o), (ɔ) | | ,, | sl*o*t.
u | = | (u) | | ,, | g*oe*d.
uu | = | (uɪ) | | ,, | b*oe*r.
ui | = | (ui) | | ,, | b*oei*.
y | = | (y) | | ,, | min*uu*t.
yy | = | (yɪ) | | ,, | z*uu*r.
yu | = | (yu) | | ,, | *uw*.

Note that 'əi' only occurs finally, and that the long high vowels 'ii,' 'uu,' and 'yy' only occur before (rr).

н	kh,gh	j	rr		s,z		bh	w	f,v
—			l						
	k,g		t,d				p,b		
—	q		n				m		

(gh) is often (generally in the province of Holland) re-tracted (ˌgh), often with a more or less marked trill. (kh) is often also (ˌkh), and in the combination (skh), as in *schip* (skhre¹p), it is often slightly trilled. (g) occurs only as a secondary modification of (k) before a voiced stop, as in 'bakboord.' (т) is the sound of *tj* and *dj*, as in *praatje* (prrɑɪтjeh), *bedje* (beɪтjeh). Similarly in *sj* (s) has the sound of (sj), as in *dasje* (dɑɪsjjeh). The glide from the preceding vowel is clearly heard in all these words, so that the effect is almost (prrɑɪɪтjeh). (rr) often becomes (ghr⸍) (l), (t), (d), (n) seem to be the same as in English, not being dental. (l) tends towards gutturality. (sh) is

heard in French words, and is an occasional sound of
Dutch *sj*, as in 'sjouwen ᵃ.' (bh), as in 'wat,' appears to
be sometimes a weak (v), as in North German ᵇ. (w),
which is narrow, is generated when a diphthong ending
in (u) is followed by a vowel, as in *nieuwe* (niweh), *eeuwen*
(eɪwehn), *blaauwe* (blɔweh). It often becomes (bh) and
even (v), which, when a voiceless consonant follows, is
devocalised, as in *gehuwd* (ghehнyft). Initial (z) and (v)
are half-voiced, (s[ʌ]) and (f[ʌ]), and often pass into (s)
and (f).

The glide from the preceding vowel on to (j) and (w) is
always made distinct, as in the colloquial pronunciations
of *Leiden* (læ[i]jeh) and *houden* (hɔ[u]weh), and in *nieuwe*,
fraaije, &c.

1. *Sentences.*

– eˈkkˑan nit bhakhteh(n) \　– hu ghaɪtehtf[ʌ]ˑan dąɪkh \
gheɪfmehehn leˈkht \　: bhɑt skheɪlty \
: hæpjeh ghutghə slaɪpeh(n) /　: heɪl ˑbhæl dɑqky \
– eˈkkˑanmehn buknˑit f[ʌ]eˈnɪdeh(n) \
– ehn stomehkhнˑæideˈnt hɔlantseˈz dœbehl stom \
– hæi keɪk oɪvehrrdeh myɪrr \
– y f[ʌ]rreˈnt kbham s[ʌ]eɪrr ląɪtteh rrœkh \
– hæi drroqks[ʌ]ehn ghlaseˈn eɪn təɪgh æhət \
: ghaɪdeh dəɪrr oɪpehndˑun \
– deh bheˈnɪdeˈz nąɪrrʌt bhæsteh(n)gheh drraɪit \
– ehn joqmænsf[ʌ]an ghu[i]jeh hæhəzeh \

ᵃ According to Donders. Land only allows (sj). Perhaps (sᴊj)
may also be heard.

ᵇ Land makes it a lip-teeth-stop, which has very much the sound
of a weak (v).

– deh kɔu maɪgddeh læhiнæido·n moɪghehlehk ˅

: eˡzehrɾi·ts ·niusf[ʌ]an dạɪkh ⁄

– [ʌ]t f[ʌ]rɾistehn sneɪut ˅

– [ʌ]t spæeitmeh s[ʌ]eɪrɾdateˡk æhətbh·as ˅

di muilehkн·æideˡz æh·əddeh(n) bhækhgheh rræhəmɪt ˅

– [ʌ]teˡs heɪl moɪi bheɪrr ˅

– hæi hɔuts[ʌ]eˡkha·ndeh ɔ[u]wehgheh bhoɪnteh(n) ˅ a

2. *Poetry (in Broad Romic)*

: hughə nughlək rɔlteht leevən

: dæsghə rəstən landmans heen

: dizən zaaləgh lɔt ⁄ – hu kleen ⁄

omgh·een koonəqsk·roon zou gheevən ˅

laaghə rəzdbra veerddən lɔf

: vaneht hookhstə koonəqshɔf ˅.

: alsən buurzən heighənd ɔsən

– ət ghliempənt koutərd·oordə klɔnt

: vanzən erfələkən ghront

: iendə lywtdər hooghə bosən

voortz it trekən ⁄   : ɔfzən ghraan

– ət veddər b klaaimet ghoudbə laadən

The ordinary spelling is: 'Ik kan niet wachten. Hoe gaat het van daag? Geef mij een licht. Wat scheelt u? Heb je goed geslapen? Heel wel, dank u. Ik kan mijn boek niet vinden. Een stommigkeit in't Hollandsch is dubbel stom. Hij keek over de muur. Uw vriend kwam zeer laat terug. Hij dronk zijn glas in één teug uit. Ga de deur open doen. De wind is naar het westen gedraaid. En jong mensch van goede huize. De koude maakt de luiheid onmogelijk. Is er iets nieuws van daag? Het vriest en sneeuwt. Het spijt mij zeer dat ik uit was. Die moeilijkheid is uit den weg geruimd. Het is heel mooi weer. Hij houdt zich aan de oude gewoonten.'

b Or 'vettər' (?).

: ɔfzən ghladə mɔləkujən
eevən ləstəkh eevən blei
ondərt ghraəzənv·antər zei
: ienən bokhtəgh dal hoort lujən ⸝
toonmə danoo armə stat
zəlkən well·əst zəlkən skhat ⸜ ᵃ

ICELANDIC.

		iı			*i*(ı)
		eı[i]	a(ı)		*eı*
		æ			
uı					*y*(ı)
oı[u]			o(ı)		*ə*(ı)

The diphthongs are :—aı[i], aı[u], eı[i], oı[u], əı[i].
The first elements are short before double consonants.
(j) after a consonant is often weakened into a vowel, and
forms a diphthong with the following vowel, as in *fé*
(f[i]eı), *vilja* (vıl[i]a). These glide-vowels may all be wide,
as it is not easy to distinguish between narrow and wide
glides.

(a) and (aı) tend towards (ą), which is the common

The ordinary spelling of the first six lines is :—

> Hoe genoeglijk rolt het leven
> des gerusten landmans heen,
> die zijn zalig lot, hoe kleen,
> om geen koningskroon zou geven !
> Lage rust braveert den lof
> van het hoogste koningshof.

sound in unaccented syllables. Short (i) is heard in the combination *ing*, as in *þíng*=(thнiqιg) or, perhaps, sometimes (thнiqιg). Short (u) occurs before *ng*, and other combinations as well, as in *úlf* (ulιv). (æ) and (e) seem to interchange, and there may perhaps be an (œ) for (ə), for which (æh) seems also to occur. There is a tendency to end (eɪ) and (oɪ) in a voice-glide, giving (eɪ[ʌ]) and (oɪ[ʌ]), which is, however, very slight. (oɪu) often becomes (oɪu). (o) and (oɪ) are sometimes lowered towards (ɔ), as in Swedish and Danish.

The high vowels always end voicelessly, the glottis being opened before the tongue is lowered, so that *í* (iɪн) and *ú* (aɪuн) sound like (iɪjh) and (aɪuwh). In the case of (u) there seems to be often a consonantal lip-narrowing at the moment of opening the glottis.

The following are the Broad Romic letters: —

a	=	(a), (ạ)	*as in*	mann*a*.
aa	=	(aɪ)	„	t*a*ka.
ai	=	(arĩ), (ai)	„	v*æ*n, b*œ*kr ; v*æ*ng.
au	=	(aɪu), (au)	„	þ*á* ; *á*tti.
e	=	(æ)	„	m*e*nn.
ee	=	(eɪ)	„	n*e*t.
ei	=	(eɪi), (ei)	„	*ei*n, r*ey*na ; *ei*nn.
ə	=	(ə)	„	sk*ö*mm.
əə	=	(əɪ)	„	f*ö*t.
əi	=	(əɪi), (əi)	„	sk*au*t ; h*au*st, l*ö*ng.
i ᵃ	=	(*i*), (i⸝)	„	m*i*nn*i*, m*y*nd ; þ*i*ng.
ii	=	(iɪ)	„	v*í*n, b*ý*li.
ie	=	(i⸍)	„	v*i*ta, f*y*rir.

Short (i) may be denoted by doubling, *ii*, leaving the shortness to be inferred from the two consonants following.

L

o	=	(*o*)	*as in*	gott.
oo	=	(oɪ)	„	kᴏma.
ou	=	(oɪu), (ou)	„	góð; ósk.
u	=	(u)	„	úng, úlf.
uu	=	(uɪ)	„	hús.
y	=	(*y*)	„	*u*pp, hús*u*m.
yy	=	(*y*ɪ)	„	m*u*n.

The consonants are :—

ʜ	(kh),gh	jh,j	rh*r*,r*r*	th,dh	s			wh,(w)	f,v
—			lh,l						
	k,g		t,d				p,b		
—	(qh),q		nh,n				(mh),m		

Those enclosed in ( ) are secondary formations, which only occur in certain combinations.

Consonants written double are pronounced double when medial. When final, double stops are long, other consonants are short.

(gh) is strongly squeezed with very little buzz, so that it closely resembles (g). Before certain vowels (all originally front), (k) and (g) become (k*ᴛ) and (g*ᴅ), written for convenience (ᴋ) and (ɢ), with simultaneous outer back and inner front stoppage. (qh) and (q) only occur before (k) and (g), never alone.

(j) is often so weak that it is not easy to distinguish it from a vowel. It seems to be generally a glide-vowel after a consonant, as in *fé* (f[i]eɪ), *fékk* (f[i]e[ʜ]kɪ), *vilja* (vɪl[i]a).

(l), (t), (n), &c. seem to be half-dental, with the tip of

the tongue on the teeth-rim. (dh) is often formed without contact, which makes the buzz almost inaudible.

For (wh) (kv) is substituted in some parts of Iceland, as in *hva*ð = (whaɪdh) or (kvaɪdh). (khw) seems also to occur.

(w) is narrow; it arises from (gh), as in *ljúga*, which through (l[i]uɪghwa) becomes (l[i]uɪwa), which is the usual pronunciation. (f) and (v) are often pronounced with feeble friction, so that (v) resembles (bh).

Initial (jh), (lh), and (nh) seem to become vocal just before the glide to the vowel begins, so that (lhaɪdha) = *hla*ð*a* sounds like (lhlaɪdha). Initial (th) is aspirated, there being an independent stress on the breath-glide, as in *þa*ð (thнaɪdh) [a].

Final (rr), (l), (n), and (m) end voicelessly, the glottis being opened just before the tongue is removed, so that (lн), as in *vel*, sounds like (llh). Final (gh), as in *dag*, becomes (ʻgh).

gg, *dd*, and *bb* are half-voiced when medial, as in *vagga* (vakk[ʌ]a). When final, as in *egg*, the off-glide seems to be whispered (ækɪ[ʻʌ]) or (æʻgɪ). *ll* is (tɪlh) when final, as in *öll*, and apparently (tɪʻl) when medial, as in *falla* [b]. Similarly *nn* after original long vowels and diphthongs is (tɪnh) and (tɪʻn). *Sag*ð*i*, *haf*ð*i*, &c., are generally pronounced either (sakɪʻdhɪ), (hapɪdhɪ), or else (in some parts) (saghɪdɪ), (havɪdɪ).

kk, *tt*, and *pp* are always preceded by a breath-glide, as in *flokk* (floнkɪ), of various degrees of force, which is the chief distinction between *kk*, &c. and *gg*, &c. when final.

This was pointed out to me by Mr. Magnusson, of Cambridge, quite lately.

[b] Perhaps (tɪlh) also.

The on-and-off glides of front consonants are very distinct. Thus *bogi* (boɪjɪ) sounds like (boɪ[i]jɪ), *gæti* (ɢaɪitɪ) like (ɢjaɪitɪ).

The following are the principal Broad Romic consonant letters :—

kh	=	kh	*as in*	a*k*ta.
kj	=	(ᴋ)	,,	*k*enna, *k*jósa.
gh	=	(gh)	,,	sa*g*a.
gj	=	(ɢ)	,,	*g*eta, *g*æti.
gk	=	(kk[ʌ]), (-ˈgɪ)	,,	va*gg*a, e*g*g.
gkj	=	(ᴋᴋ[ʌ])	,,	li*gg*ja.
qh	=	(qh)	,,	lá*ng*t.
jh	=	(jh)	,,	*hj*á.
rh	=	(rh*r*)	,,	*h*ríng, ha*r*t.
lh	=	(lh)	,,	*hl*aða, bi*l*t.
dt	=	(tt[ʌ]), (-ˈdɪ)	,,	ho*dd*um, o*dd*.
nh	=	(nh)	,,	*h*nut, *k*níf, bei*n*t.
mh	=	(mh)	,,	ja*f*nt (jamht).
bp	=	(pp[ʌ]), (-ˈbɪ)	,,	ga*bb*a, ga*bb*.

A. Prose.

1. *Old Icelandic.*

– hin thrrɪɪdhi ausærrs·auærr katɪˈladhyrrærr ·n[i]ərr dhyrr ⟨

– han bɪɪrrau himɪnɪ⁄ : thaɪrrsæm heɪitɪrr noɪ[u]wat· uɪn ⟨

– han rraɪidhyrrf·ɪɪrrɪrr gəiqɪgy vɪnɪs⁄ – ok stɪtɪˈlɪrr s[i]aɪuok ælɪd ⟨

– au hanskal heɪitatɪl saɪif·aɪrraoktɪl veɪidha ⟨.

: hanærrsvau əɪidhighyrrokf[i]eɪs·aitlh ⁄

−atʜ·anmau ɢeɪva theɪim əɪidh lanɪdaeɪ·dhyrr ləɪisaf
[i]aɪurr ⁄
− ærrauʜan heɪitatɪlth·æs ᐸ
: hanvarr y[ʜ]pɪf·aitt[ʌ]yrri vaɪnaʜ·eɪimym ⁄
− æn vaɪnɪrr ɢislydhyh·an gɔɪdhynym ⁄
− ok tɔɪukyi mɔɪutat aɪusaɢ·isliqɪgyth·anærr haɪinɪrr
heɪitɪrr ᐸ
− hanv·arrdhat sai[ʜ]tɪmædh gɔɪdhynymokvəɪnym ᐸ
n[i]ərrdhyrrau thaɪu kɔɪnyærr ·skaɪdhi heɪitirr ᐸ
dou[ʜ]ttɪrr th[i]assa jəɪtyns ᐸ
skaɪdhivɪlʜ·aɪva buɪst·aɪdh thanærr au[ʜ]tʜapɪ·dhi
faɪdhɪrrʜ·ænnarr ᐸ
: thaɪtærrau f[i]ətɪlym nə[ʜ]kɪvorrymth aɪrrsæm heɪitɪrr
thrryɪmʜ·eɪimyrr ᐸ
− æn n[i]ərrdhyrrv·il veɪrran·aɪirr saɪi ᐸ
− thəigh sai[ʜ]ttystau thaɪt ⁄
: atthəighs·ʀɪlidy veɪrra niɪyᵃ naɪityrri thrryɪmh·eɪimi ⁄
− ænthau aɪdhrrarr niɪyat nɔɪ[u]wat·uɪnym ᐸ
− ænæ·rr n[i]ərrdhyrrkɔɪm aftyrrtɪl nɔɪ[u]wat·uɪnaav
f[i]atɪ·liny ⁄
− thau kvaɪdhhan th[ʜ]ætta ᐸ
    leɪidheɪ·rrymk f[i]ətɪlh ᐸ
    varhrkaæk leiqɪɢi ᐸ
    naɪityrr eɪinarr niɪy ᐸ
    ulva th[ʜ]iɪtyrr
    m[i]eɪrr th[ʜ]ou[ʜ]tti itɪ·lyrrv·eɪrra
    : jhau səiqɪgvi svaɪna ᐸ
− thau kvaɪdh skaɪdhi th[ʜ]ætta ᐸ
    sɔɪvaæk mau[ʜ]ttat
    saɪivarr bædh[i]ym au
    fykɪ·ls jarrmi fiɪrrirr ᐸ
         Not diphthongic.

: saɪumɪ̄k veɪkᴜrr

: æɪrrav viɪdhɪ ᴋeɪmᴜrr

morrgyn whærr[i]an maɪurr \

– thau foɪurr skaɪdhɪ y[н]pɪau f[i]atrˈlɪt /

– ok bɪkɪˈdhɪï thrrɪmhˈeɪimɪ \

– ok færrнon m[i]əɪkau skɪɪdhymokmædh boɪgha /

– ok skɪɪtyrr diɪrr \

– hon heɪitɪrr ənɪdyrrgˈvyɪdheɪ dhᴜrr ənɪdyrrdˈiɪs \ [a]

2. *Modern Icelandic (in Broad Romic).*

(Unaccented *ii* = (i).)

– ii gammla daagha /

: fierir mərgym hyndrydh aurym /

bjoumˈjəəgh riikyr boundi–ii sailiqgsdaalstˈuqgy \.

– han autti nokkyr bədtnh /

– o(gh)eeˈry tilnˈemdir tveir sienir \.

ekkji vietamˈen whaadhthˈeir jheety /

– o kədtlymvjerthauthˈvii adtnouro svein \.

– theirvˈoory baudhir ebpnilei–ir menenthˈou oulˈiikjir \

---

[a] The following is the ordinary spelling of the beginning of the text :—

> Hinn þriði Áss er sá er kallaðr er Njörðr;
> hann býr á himni, þar sem heitir Nóatún;
> hann ræðr fyrir göngu vinds, ok stillir sjá ok eld;
> á hann skal heita til sæfara ok til veiða.
> Hann er svá auðigr ok fésæll,
> at hann má gefa þeim auð landa eðr lausafjár
> er á hann heita til þess.
> Hann var uppfœddr í Vanaheimum,
> en Vanir gisluðu hann goðunum,
> ok tóku í mót at Ásagíslíngu þann er Hœnir heitir;
> hann varð at sætt með goðunum ok Vönum.

adtnourvar hreistim·aadhyro miekjidtlf·ierir ‚sjeer ⟍
sveidtnvar haighyro spaakyro eiqgjin hreistimaadhyr⟍
: eftir thviiv·oorytheir mjəəgh oul·iikjirii lynd ⟍
adtnourvar gleedhim·aadhyr ⟍
− o gaavsighadh leikjymmedh sveinym thaarur daa-
lnym ⟍
− o mailhtytheiro·ft moutmedh sjeervidh staapa than ∕
− er stendyr niedhyrvidh auna ∕
ands·painis bainymii tuqgy ∕
− sem kadtladhyrer tuqgys·taapi ⟍.
: vaarthadh skjemtynth·eirra−au veetrym ∕
− adh rennasjeereftir hardhf·ennin·iedhyrav staapanym ∕
: thviihaner haur mjəəgh ∕
: o niedhyrau eiradtnarii kriqg ⟍.
: gjekk ᵃ oft miekjidh ·aumedh kadtlo haur·eisti
kriqgym tuqgystaapa−ii rəkkrynym ⟍ ᵃ
: ovar adtnourth·aar oftast fremstyrii flokkji ⟍ ᵇ

B. Poetry.

1. *Old Icelandic.*

s[i]eɪrɾhon 𝑦[ʜ]pɪk·oɪma	Sér hon uppkoma
ədhrɾy sinni	öðru sinni
jərɾdhorɾ aɪ[i]ji	jörð or œgi
idh[i]ag·rɾaɪina ⟍	iðjagrœna :

ᵃ = (kɪ).

ᵇ The ordinary spelling of the beginning is :—

Í gamla daga, fyɪir mörgum hundruð árum, bjó mjög ríkur bóndi
í Sælíngsdalstungu ; hann átti nokkur börn, og eru til nefndir tveir
synir. Ekki vita menn hvað þeir·hètu, og köllum vèr þá því Arnór
og Svein.

fatɪˈla fossarr ɪ   falla forsar,
fliɪghyrr ətɪˈn ɪivɪrr   flýgr örn yfir,
: saɪuærrau f[i]atɪˈli   sá er á fjalli
fɪska veɪidhɪrr \   fiska veiðir.

jheɪrr stænɪdyrr baлɪdrrɪ Hér stendr Baldri
– ov brryкк[ʌ]ɪn m[i]əɪdhyrr of bruggin mjöðr,
sкɪɪrrarr veɪigharr   skírar veigar,
lɪkk[ʌ]yrr sкəлɪdyrr ɪivɪrr \ liggr skjöldr yfir;
– æn aɪusmˈeɪ[i]ɪrr   en ásmegir
– i oɪvvˈaɪinɪ \   í ofvæni;
nəɪidhygh sakɪˈdhak \   nauðug sagðak,
nuɪmˈyɪnæk th[н]eɪ[i]a \   nu mun ek þegja.

f[i]eɪok f[i]ərrvɪ   Fé ok fjörvi
rrainhtɪ fɪrrdha кɪnɪd   rænti fyrða kind
: sauнɪn grrɪmmɪ grræ[н]ppyrr \ sá hinn grimmi greppr
: ɪivɪrthau gəɪty   yfir þá götu,
: ærrнan varrdhadhɪ   er hann varðaði,
naɪudhɪ eiqɪGɪ kvɪikyrr   náði eingi kvikr
    koɪmask \   komask.

2. *Modern Icelandic (in Broad Romic).*

– ii morgynroodhans mindym
   myynadhu broosir viedh \
   sviivyrmedh syymarvˈindym
   siiqgyrii fygkla kliedh \
– au beedhi bloumgra stranda
– migh bliidhast dreimir nhos \
   kvəldvˈindaraˈdhmjeer anda
   : ou siinileghrar kos \

SWEDISH.

		ɯ			i
	eh	e(ɪ)	a	ẹh[i]	e(ɪ)
		æ(ɪ)	aɪ		
	uhɪ	yɪ		uh	y
oˡ(ɪ)					ə(ɪ)
ɔˡɪ		œ(ɪ)	ɔˡ		

The diphthongs are :—ẹh[i], o[i], ə[i], besides (a[i]) and (a[uh]), which only occur in foreign words.

(a) tends to (ạ), especially in unaccented syllables. (æ) and (œ), both long and short, interchange with (e) and (ə) : they are commonest before (r). (i) and (y) are very close, so that they are very like (i) and (y). (oˡ) is (o)+ rounding of (u), and (ɔˡ) is (ɔ)+rounding of (o). Note that the (ˡ) in this case is not meant to imply any *raising* of the tongue, but simply a narrowing of the lip opening. For (əɪ) (əɪ) also occurs.

The Broad Romic letters are :—

a	=	(a), (ạ)	*as in*	fall*a*.
aa	=	(aɪ)	„	t*a*ga.
ai	=	(a*i*)	„	M*a*j.
au	=	(a*u*h)	„	*Au*gusti.
æ	=	(æ), (e)	„	h*e*rre, en v*ä*n.
ae	=	(æɪ), (eɪ)	„	b*e*ra, *ä*ta.
e	=	e	„	sk*e*pp.
ee	=	eɪ	„	st*e*n.
ei	=	(ẹh*i*)	„	n*ej*, m*ig*.

ə	=	(ə), (œ); (eh)	*as in*	röst, först; vill*e*.
əə	=	(əɪ), (œɪ)	„	snö, smör.
əi	=	(ə*i*)	„	fröjd.
i	=	(*i*)	„	t*i*ng.
ii	=	(iɪ)	„	v*i*n.
o	=	(o¹)	„	h*o*n, f*o*ster.
oo	=	(o¹ɪ)	„	s*o*l.
ɔ	=	(ɔ¹)	„	k*o*mma, lång.
ao	=	(ɔ¹ɪ)	„	gå, k*o*nung.
oi	=	(ɔ¹*i*)	„	st*o*j.
u	=	(*u*h)	„	*u*ng.
uu	=	(uhi)	„	*u*t.
y	=	(*y*)	„	l*y*cka.
yy	=	(yɪ)	„	n*y*.

H		j	r		s	sh			f,v
—			l						
	k,g		t,d				p,b		
—	q		n				m		

The Swedish consonant system is, as far as it goes, identical with the English. English and Swedish are the only Teutonic languages that have final voiced stops. (l), (t), (d), and (n) appear, however, to be dental or half-dental. (r) is trilled at the beginning of a stress syllable, as in *rik*. After a long vowel, as in *far, fara*, it is generally untrilled; and when a consonant follows, as in *barn, gård*, it is so weak and short as to be almost inaudible to a foreign ear. After short vowels it is trilled, often only weakly, as in *förra, barm*. The soft *k* in *kenna* is generally identified with the English (tsh), but it appears sometimes to be (ɹjh), the forward variety of which is hardly distinguishable from (tsh). Soft *g*, as in *göra*, is generally identified with (j), but it is often (ᴅj) [a].

Voiceless stops are often joined by breath-glides, as in *akta* (ak[ʜ]ta). Final high vowels often end voicelessly, as in Icelandic, and before voiceless consonants the effect is nearly that of the corresponding breath consonant, thus (huhɪs) = *hus* becomes nearly (huhɪwhs). But these de-vocalisations are not universal.

Written double consonants are pronounced double medially. Finally all consonants are lengthened after short vowels, as in English.

The most characteristic feature of Swedish is its word-tone. Every word in Swedish has one of two tones—the compound and the simple [b]. The simple tone seems to have been originally a rise (ⵏ), but it is practically merely the negation of the compound tone, and may therefore be either a rise or a fall according to the context. The compound tone, which only occurs in words of more than one syllable, consists of a falling tone on the first (the accented syllable), followed by a high tone on the next. This high tone seems to be reached by a leap rather than by a glide. The compound is, therefore, a compound rise distributed over two syllables. It is indicated by (v) before the accented syllable on which it begins, and always strongly lengthens the consonant of that syllable, unless the vowel is long, as in *landa* (ᴠlanɪda), *dofta* (ᴠdɔˡfɪta).

[a] I have often heard this (ᴅ), but as it is ignored by the Swedes themselves, it is impossible without long observation to determine its use.

[b] See Professor Storm's article ' Om Tonefaldet,' in the Christiania Videnskabs-Selskabs Forhandlinger for 1874.

There is generally a half-strong (secondary) stress on the high-tone syllable.

These word-tones are crossed in a peculiar and complicated way by the sentence-tones common to language generally. In compound-toned dissyllables there is often no distinction made between assertion and interrogation : thus 'talar hann Svenska ?' and 'hann talar Svenska' are (taɪlarнan vsvenɪska) and (−han vtalar vsvenɪska), ending with the same tone in both cases. When another syllable follows the high-tone one, the high tone can either be continued upwards or downwards. Thus, such a word as *tilfälligtvis* may be pronounced either (vtˑɪ̆lɪf:ellɪ̆ktviis ⁄) with the high tone on the second syllable continued upwards, or (vtˑɪ̆lɪf:ellɪ̆ktviis ⁀) with a falling tone beginning on the high tone. In this way interrogative and assertive sentences may be distinguished as in other languages, and even in dissyllables it is possible to distinguish between (vsvenska ⁄) and (vsvenska ⁀).

The interval of the compound tone varies according to the emphasis with which the word is uttered.

A. Sentences.

: jaskalvɑɪra–*i* stɑɪnehtpˑɑɪr [a] vvekkɔ¹r.
devareht varrbˑeɪteh. vveɪdrᵣehtæ(r) vvakkehrt.
: frrɔ¹ɪn valɪla værɪdehns vdeɪlar.
: jafœr stɔ¹ɪrnær ˑvanɪdrᵣa tɑɪla.
tiɪd(eh)næ(r) o¹nɪd. : hanbeh fanɪsehɪ̆i stoˑ¹ɪrtbeh ho¹ɪv.
lɔ¹ɪtɔ¹s gɔ¹ɪ. − go¹ vmɔ¹rrɔ¹nmɪn vhærreh.
−han toˑ¹ɪgнɔ¹nɔ¹mɪ̆sɪt huhɪs.
vviɪsamehɪ̆tˑɪ̆lmɪ̆t rrᵤhmɪ.

[a] Or etpˑaɪr.

: jaharfœr tshyıltmeh*i*. nubeh j*y*nteheht n*y*t ѵtıɪdeh-
varѵ.

ѵmenınıshanæ(r) fədıt*i*l ѵarʀb eıteh — ɔ¹uhıtanbeh məı-
dandeh vinnehs ѵiqıehn ѵfʀramıgɔ¹q.

: kanнern ѵseh[*i*]jameh*i*var ·pɔ¹stehnæ(r).

— vif·ɔ¹ıreh*i* ѵdrʀə[*i*]ja.

English Translation.

: aishəl steiendhə taunə fyuw wiyx ѵ
thætwəzə lcibə ѵ. — dhə wedhɔz fain ѵ
— frəm aol kwaotəzəvdhə gloub ѵ
— aiə·ndə stændwhen ədhəz spiyk ѵ
— dhə taimza bæd ѵ. — hiy faundems·elfen greit streits ѵ
: lets gou ѵ. : gud maoneqs·əə ѵ
— hiy tukemi·ntuez haus ѵ
shoumitu·mai rum ѵ
— aiv kaot kould ѵ. naube gænə nyuw piiriəd ѵ
mænez baonfə ·toil : əndwedh auteg zəəshən nou
prougresezə teind ѵ
: kænyuw telmiy whaeədhə poustao fesi·s /
: wiy məsnt weit ѵ

B. Prose (*in Broad Romic*).

həstəni noordənhaaren ᵃ ѵstilla juupmel·aqko lii ѵ
— mænde ѵeevikt ѵgrəəna graanɔ ѵfuuruskoogarnə /
— sɔm ѵkrəənadæs bærjɔ ѵhəidər / — ɔsɔm ѵsuusa
ѵliika ѵfriska /
— ɔm ѵsɔmmarns ѵflæktarɔ ѵfaoglar ѵleeka–id æm /
— æ·l(l)ərɔmd eeras shæg ѵflyygafœr ѵnoordanstɔrmən /
— maedan ѵkɔrparna ѵkretsaii shyyn ѵ

(e) or (eh).

– dæssa vskoogartˑaaga bɔrt alt bleekt ⁄
alt veektɔ vmjæltshuuktfraon vveemoodət \
– ɔ vjiivadae(t)en vstæmpəlav vhəəgheetɔ vjuupsinnikt
valvaar \.
– dæn vgamla vvaalan vandasundər vsɔrjəsləian \.
– ɔsˑao vkɔmma–aevən vdaagar ⁄
vhærliga vdaagar ⁄
– dao vtaltrastən shuqəriidən vfrɔstklaara vmɔrgɔnən \
– dao vhəəgmaolnən staoi vpurpurɔ guldəəvərde
vduqkəlgrəəna vhəidərna \
– dao luftənær vspænstigɔ læt \
lætsɔmen vflyygandə faogəl \
– ɔ vmænnishans krɔpɔ vsinnən vliikasɔmbə viqasdær
aav \
vdaagardao soolən lyysəri vreenastə glansəəvərdən
vbrookiga joordən \
– dær ləəvən vguulnatɔ vrəndruuvan gləədər \
– dao vnɔrsheenən vflamma–i kvællən \
– ɔ daoærdæ vhærliktii noordən \

C. Poetry.

(1)

: dæɪr vveksteh vuhɪti vhɪ̄lɪdɪqs gɔ¹ɪrd \
: tvɔ¹ɪ vplanɪtɔ¹ruˑhnɪdehr vfo¹strarns vɔ¹ɪrd \
– ehi no¹ɪrdehn fœɪɪ setɪ tvɔ¹ɪsɔ¹ vshəɪna
– de vveksteh vhærɪlɪ̄ktide(t) vgrrəɪna.

– den veɪnasˑɔ¹men ˑeɪk shəɪt frramɪ \
– ɔ¹sˑɔ¹men ˑlanɪserнˑen(n)ehs stamɪ \
– men ˑvkrro¹ɪnansɔ¹mi vɪ̄nɪdehn shelɪvehr
– lɪ̄ksɔ¹men ˑjelɪmsɪ̄n vruhnɪdehl velɪvehr \.

− den vanɪdrʀa ʋʋe' stehs·ɔ¹men rro¹ɪs
: næɪr vɪntehrn nysʜar flytɪsɪn ko¹ɪs
: men vɔ¹ɪrehns·ɔ¹mden rro¹ɪsehn jəmmehr
: i knɔ¹ppehn lɪggehr enɪɔ¹ drrəmmehr ʋ.

− men stɔ¹rrmehn skalk·rrɪq jo¹ɪrdehn gɔ¹ɪ
− medʜ·ɔ¹nɔ¹m ʋbrrɔ¹tɪtas eɪkehn dɔ¹ɪ
− ɔ¹ ʋʋɔ¹ɪrs·o¹ɪlsk·alpɔ¹ ʋhɪmɪlehn ʋglɑɪda
− dɔ¹ vəpɪnar rro¹ɪsehn ʋlepɪpar ʋrrɑɪda ᵃ.

2. (*In Broad Romic*).

: see ʋfaoglarnəs ʋskaara
− til ʋfræmmandə land
− de ʋsukkandə ʋfaara
− fraon ʋgautjoods strand ʋ
− mæd vaedrənde ʋblanda
− sit ʋklaagandə juud ʋ.
: vaar ʋskoolavi ʋlanda
: vart fəərɔsdit buud ʋ.
− sɔ ʋroopardæn ʋfj·aedradə ʋskaarantil guud ʋ

− vii ʋlæmnamæd ʋoor·oo
− de skandiska shaer ʋ

ᵃ The ordinary spelling of the first two stanzas is :—
    Der växte uti Hildings gård
    två plantor under fostrarns vård.
    Ej Norden förr sett två så sköna,
    de växte herrligt i det gröna.

    Den ena som en ek sköt fram,
    och som en lans är hennes stam,
    men kronan, som i vinden skälfver,
    liksom en hjelm sin rundel hvälfver.

− vii ѵtriivdəsvii ѵѵooro
− sɔ ѵˑlykliga daer\.
− ii ѵblommandə ѵlindar
: daer ѵnæstətvii bykt
− bal saamiska ѵѵindar
− ɔs ѵѵaggadə trykt \.
: nuu strækkəsm oot ѵoocænda ѵrymdərѵaor flykt \

: ѵaad ѵjəəravii ѵlæqrə
− i noordən \   : dæs pool
: bliir ѵdaagligən ѵtræqrə
: meer duqkəldæs sool \.
: ѵaad ѵbaotarat ѵkviida
− vi ѵlæmnaen graav \
− at flyyidæ ѵѵiida
guud ѵѵiqarɔs gaav \
− sao ѵaarənɔs ѵhælsade ѵbruusandə haav \

DANISH [a].

		i(ɪ)			*i*
	eh	e(ɪ)	a̡(ɪ)		eɪ
		æ			
u(ɪ)		y(ɪ)			*y*
oˡ(ɪ)		ə(ɪ)			əɪ
ɔˡɪ		œ	ɔˡ		

The diphthongs are :—a̡[*i*], a̡[oˡ], and ɔˡ[*i*] [b]. The first elements are always short.

Observe the delicate distinctions of the front vowels, and the same abnormal rounding of the back vowels as in Swedish.

(e) is always very close = (eˡ). So also (ə). The forwardness of (a̡) is very marked, especially when long and when unaccented. In vulgar speech it seems often to pass quite into (æ). (æ) and (œ) are not very low, and may perhaps interchange with (e) and (ə).

Final high vowels end voicelessly, as in Icelandic.

The Broad Romic letters are :—

a	=	(a̡)	*as in*	en mand.
aa	=	(a̡ɪ)	,,	at mane.
æ	=	(æ)	,,	en hest.

[a] Compare my paper on Danish Pronunciation,' in the Trans. of the Philological Society, 1873-4.

[b] I am not certain of the exact character of the second elements, as I formerly regarded them as consonants.

M

ae	=	(eɪ)	*as in*	et træ.
ai	=	(aɨ)	,,	jeg.
ao	=	(ɔ¹ɪ)	,,	en maane.
au	=	(ąo¹)	,,	et navn.
e	=	(e)	,,	hende, bredt.
ee	=	(eɪ)	,,	bred.
ə	=	(ə), (eh)	,,	först, at give.
əə	=	(əɪ)	,,	en sö.
i	=	(i)	,,	gik, hvidt.
ii	=	(iɪ)	,,	hvid.
ie	=	(ɨ)	,,	fik, at finde.
o	=	(o¹)	,,	et gods, ung.
oo	=	(o¹ɪ)	,,	god.
œ	=	(œ)	,,	störst.
oe	=	(əɪ)	,,	en dör.
oi	=	(ɔ¹ɨ)	,,	et öje.
ɔ	=	(ɔ¹)	,,	et folk, maatte.
y	=	(y)	,,	en skyld, nydt.
yy	=	(yɪ)	,,	at nyde.
ye	=	(y)	,,	at skylle.

ʀ,ʜ	(jh), j	gh		thj, dhj	s	sh			f, v
—			(lh), l						
x		k, g	t, d				p, b		
—		q	(nh), n				m		

Those in ( ) are secondary formations.

Observe the full development of the throat-sounds, and the numerous varieties of point and blade consonants, as in English.

The (ʀ) is really (ʀ) + (ghw), or, in other words, an

English (w) with the tongue retracted + (ʀ). There is also a secondary voiceless form. The (ʀ)-narrowing is generally carried into the following vowel, to which, if it is front, it communicates something of a back quality. Hence *bröd* (bʀəɪxˈdh) has to an English ear the effect of ' broidh.'

The glottal catch (x), or 'stödtone' (s·t[ʌ]ədhjtʜːoˡɪneh), corresponds to the ' simple tone' in Swedish, the Swedish ' compound tone' being represented by the absence of the (x). The (x) always follows its vowel, which it shortens somewhat when long. (gh) often becomes (ghw) after back-round vowels, as in *suge* (suɪghweh), which becomes (suuweh) and then (suueh), and in *og* (əˡghw), which also drops its consonant in rapid speech, becoming (əˡ). After front vowels (gh) is also often dropped, as in *sige* = (suɪˌgheh) or (suɪeh). (l), (t), &c. seem to be half-dental. (thj) and (dhj) are formed without contact, and often become almost inaudible.

Voiceless stops at the beginning of a stress syllable are aspirated, except when (s) precedes them. When not aspirated they are half-voiced, except, of course, finally. Examples are *til* (tʜiˈl), *stille* (st[ʌ]ileh), *ikke* (ik[ʌ]eh), *skat* (sk[ʌ]at). If a voiced consonant follows an aspirated stop the aspiration passes into it, and it becomes voiceless, as in *klokke* (klhəˡk[ʌ]eh).

All final consonants, unless already voiceless, are whispered, as also is (gh) before a voiceless consonant, as in *magt* (maˈght).

All final consonants are short. Vowel-like consonants before voiced consonants are long, but if (x) precedes, they are short and whispered, as in *mandel* (max'ndehl). The second elements of diphthongs, when followed

by voiced consonants, are lengthened into full vowels,
but without taking a fresh stress-impulse, as in *sejle.*
This effect is best represented by (sa[*i*]*ii*leh), implying
$\overline{\text{(sa}[i]ii\text{-leh})}$.

The chief Broad Romic consonant letters that require
to be noted are :—

dh	=	(dh*j*)	*as in*	gu*d.*
gh	=	(gh), (gh*w*)	,,	da*g*e, o*g.*
jh	=	(jh)	,,	*tj*ene.
kh	=	(kʜ)	,,	*k*omme.
lh	=	(lh)	,,	k*l*okke.
nh	=	(nh)	,,	*kn*æ.
ph	=	(pʜ)	,,	*p*enge.
r	=	(ʀ)	,,	*r*et.
rh	=	(ʀh)	,,	t*r*æt.
sh	=	(sh)	,,	*sj*æl.
th	=	(th*j*)	,,	lande*t.*
th	=	(tʜ)	,,	*t*age.
x	=	(x)	,,	*s*e.

In the following specimens the laryngal *r* is written
simply (ʀ). (ạ) is written simply (a). Long vowels which
have not the full stress are half-long, as usual.

A. Sᴇɴᴛᴇɴᴄᴇs.

:hanehrehn slæx‘m o¹ıx‘n max‘n \. :dæʀehs uıx‘ʀgɔ¹ıʀ-
al deıxlehs faɪx‘l \
 —hun ʀakt[ʌ]ehʜa‘m hɔ¹xnıtʜ*i*l tʜaɪx‘npʜɔ¹fɔ¹ʀ sɔ¹ıxn*i*‘q\
:hanfɔ¹‘ʀ tjhæxnehʀ *i*qın beıdhj̇ʀeh sk[ʌ]eıpneh \ ᵃ

 ᵃ (pɴ) without any breath-glide after the (p).

oˡnsk[ʌ]ylaja tʜaɪʀmaɪdn friʜeɪdhja gəɪʀehdemeht səˡdnt
sp[ʌ]œˈʀsmɔˡɪxˈl\

– han aoˡʜˈəˡxˈltsaɪfˈʀaa(t) ytʀehsin meɪnɪq∕ – a fʀyˈght-
fəˡʀafəˡʀ næxʀmehʜam \

siɪxˈghtʜɪl kʜusk[ʌ]ehnaʜanɪˈk[ʌ]ehməˡ kʜəɪʀeh altfəˡʀ
laqsəˡmt \

: det[ʌ]eh oˡɪxʀ bʀuɪghwehs shæliˈn \

: gœʀ ɪk[ʌ]ehmˈiɪneh st[ʌ]əvlehʀ altfəˡʀ sneɪvʀehəˡoˡehʀ
vʀɪstˈn \

devˈilehʜan ɪk[ʌ]ehsˈiɪ(gh)eh naɪtˈʜɪˈl\   .tʜak sk[ʌ]al-
du ha \

: jaɪhaʀnˈæstn ɪk[ʌ]eh loˡk[ʌ]ehthjmˈiɪneh əˡ[ɪ]ɪmehdn
heɪleh nat \

– han ʀaɪsteh heɪleh veɪʀɪdn ʀoˡxˈnt \
skʀiɪxvehʀʜan [a] æxqehlsk ∕

The ordinary spelling is :—

Han er en slem ond Mand.   Deres Uhr gaaer aldeles
fejl.

Hun rakte ham Haanden til Tegn paa Forsoning.

Han fortjener ingen bedre Skjæbne.

Undskyld at jeg tager mig den Frihed, at göre Dem
et saadant Spörgsmaal.

Han afholdt sig fra at ytre sin Mening, af Frygt for
at fornærme ham.

Sig til Kudsken, at han ikke maa kjöre altfor langsomt.

Dette Ord bruges sjelden.

Gjör ikke mine Stövler altfor snævre over Vristen.

Det vilde han ikke sige Nei til.   Tak skal Du have.

Jeg har næsten ikke lukket mine Öjne den hele Nat.

---

[a] (skʀ) without any breath-glide after the (k).

Han rejste hele Verden rundt.
Skriver han Engelsk?

B. Prose.

heɪleh uɪghʍehni gæxnehmm·ɔt[ʌ]eh lileh klhao¹xs
plhɔ¹ɪehfɔ¹ʀ st[ʌ]o¹ɪʀeh klhao¹xs /

— ɔ¹ lɔ¹ɪnehʜamsin eɪnehst[ʌ]eh hæst \

— sɔ¹ jaxlp st[ʌ]o¹ɪʀeh klhao¹xsʜami gænme alehs iɪneh
fiɪʀeh \

— men kʜo¹n eɪxngaxqɔ¹m uɪghʍehn \

— ɔ¹ devaʀɔ¹ʿm sœxʿndaɪghehʿn \.

·husa \ — vo¹ʀ smælehdhʲeh lileh klhao¹xsmesin pʜisk-
ɔ¹o¹ehʀ aleh fæxʿm hæsteh \

— de vaʀjo¹n·usɔ¹ gɔ¹tsɔ¹m haxns / dæxn eɪneh daɪxʿgh \.
so¹ɪxlehn sk[ʌ]ɪnehdhʲehsɔ¹ daɪli(gh) \

— ɔ¹ aleh klhɔ¹k[ʌ]ehʀi kʜɪ́ʀk[ʌ]ehtɔ¹ɪxʀnehthʲ ʀiqeh-
dhʲehtʜɪl kʜɪ́ʀk[ʌ]eh \

fɔ¹xʿlkvaʀsɔ¹ pʜyntehdhʲeh \

— ɔ¹ gikme salmehb·ɔ¹ɪxghoʹnehʀaɪʿxʿʀmehn hæxn /

— ahɔɪʀeh pʀhæstn ᵃ pʀheɪk[ʌ]eh \

— ɔ¹di sɔ¹ɪxpʜɔ¹ lileh klhao¹xs \

— deʀ plhɔ¹ɪehdhʲehme fæxm hæsteh \

: ʜanv·aʀsɔ¹fɔ¹ʀ nɔ¹ɪxehthʲ /

: aʜan smælehdhʲehi gænme pʜiskehnɔ¹ ʀɔ¹pteh \

·hyp alehm·iɪneh hæsteh \

ᵃ No breath-glide from the (t) to the (n).

C. Poetry (in Broad Romic).

(1)

− du vandrieqs maxnvedh səəxən
− o staxnsdin raskə gaxq \
sæxn bliekəthɔˑuər əəxən
− ɔ həəxrmin mienəsaxq \
væxn daexrhænd·iinə thaqkər
− din læxqsələdin sɔxrgh \
− phɔ hiinə guulə baqkər
stooxdh foexrən ridhərbˑɔxrgh \

− i læxqstfɔr svoxnnə daaghə
: vardəni glaxnsɔ maght \
nuærdər knhapthiel baaghə
− ru iixnəra(u)dns prhaght \
mæni·di gamlə thiidhər
− dav·ardn hoixɔ stooxr \
− ɔ saoxsthiel alə siidhər /
− ɔ knhaisədhəfra jooxr \

− dæn iekə mɔnə vaerə
− fɔr nooghən vikieq byght \
− u raanjathiel aerə
− dæn raistəsaisɔ trhyght \
− fra mænəskənəs vriemlən
− vedh haaxvəth skiexltdæn laox /
− ɔ haevədhsaimoodh hiemlən
− ɔ mooxdhdi stjærnər smaox \

(2)

hærlighə moodhər skjɔlm·əəx prhuuxdh /
gjoorətha(u) haaxvəths səlb·laox bæltə /
hist klaexti graanərs sɔrghdoxqklə skruuxdh /
skygəth haexra(u) lyysg·rœnə thæltə /
steexnærdit phansər \
iisb raexdin jæxlmɔ skaexrdiinə lansər \
malmtoqə seenər snooxdin aaxrm \
: mæn khaermienərnə smyekədin baaxrm
— ɔd in iesəpo laaxrs·tjaernən krhansər \

APPENDIX.

THE PRINCIPLES OF SPELLING REFORM.

INTRODUCTION.

THE absolute necessity of phonetic reform is now almost universally recognised, not only by practical teachers but also by scientific philologists. All the objections that prejudice and irrational conservatism have been able to devise have been successfully met, and the only question now is, What system shall we adopt?

The great difficulty of arriving at any agreement is the multiplicity of possible systems. Any system, however clumsy and arbitrary, which clears away only a portion of the irregularities of the existing spelling, is an improvement on it. Any one, for instance, if he likes, can drop the silent *w* in such words as *write*, and make *night* into *nite*, thus getting rid of a large number of irregularities at one stroke. In fact, given a hundred human beings of average intellect who can read and write, it would be perfectly easy to turn out a hundred different systems of spelling, all of them more or less an improvement on the existing one.

This was until lately the state of things—every man did what was right in his own eyes. But in the thirty years that have elapsed since Messrs. Ellis and Pitman first began to work a phonetic alphabet, practically everything has been changed, especially within the last ten years. The labours of Messrs. Bell and Ellis have given us a thorough analysis of the sounds of English, the history of English pronunciation has been fully investigated by Mr. Ellis, and a variety of spellings have been practically tested.

It is now possible from an examination of these various systems to deduce certain general principles, by which all reform must be guided. If there were no such principles, the problem would be a hopeless one. Nothing can be done without unanimity, and until the majority of the community are convinced of the superiority of some one system, unanimity is impossible.

No one is qualified to give an opinion on spelling reform who has not studied these general principles, and has at least an elementary knowledge of the formation of the sounds of the English language and their relations to one another.

The present remarks are intended to supply the necessary information in as clear and untechnical a form as possible, so as to enable the general reader to form an independent judgment without having to search through an indefinite number of scattered publications.

GENERAL PRINCIPLES.

Choice of Letters.

The object of an alphabet being to represent to the eye the sounds of a language by means of written symbols, it follows that in a rational alphabet—

(1) Every simple sound must have a distinct symbol, and

(2) There must be a definite relation between each sound and its symbol.

These principles are carried out in Mr. Bell's ' Visible Speech.' In this alphabet each letter symbolises the action of the vocal organs by which it is formed, according to certain fixed principles. Thus, all consonants are symbolised by a curve, like a c, which is turned in different directions to indicate the place in the mouth where each consonant is formed. ᴜ , for instance, indicates any consonant formed by the point of the tongue, such as *t, d,* or *l*; ᴐ, one formed by the lips, such as *p, b,* or *m.* The different varieties of ' point- ', ' lip- ', &c. consonants are indicated by modifiers added to these fundamental symbols. A short straight line inside the curve converts voiceless (surd) consonants, such as *t, p, s,* into the corresponding voiced (sonant) consonants *d, b, z,* &c. A bar across the opening of the curve denotes a ' shut ' consonant or mute. So that any one who knows the symbols for *t* and *d* is at once able to recognise the symbol of *b* if he knows that of *p.*

Such an alphabet is, to a great extent, *self-interpreting.* When the meaning of a few radical signs have been learnt, hundreds of letters are understood at once, without further explanation. It is also a *universal alphabet,* providing symbols not only for all existing, but also for all possible sounds.

The Roman alphabet, with which English and most other European languages are written, evidently falls far short of this standard. In the first place, its letters are formed quite arbitrarily, and bear no definite relation to the sounds they indicate. No one would infer, for instance, from the shape of the letters that *d* was nearly related to *t,* and that there was the same relation between *b* and *p.* Again, the Roman alphabet supplies an utterly inadequate number of symbols for the sounds of most languages. Although the original alphabet has been supplemented in modern times by the addition of such letters as *j, v,* and *w,* it is still very defective, and consequently distinct sounds are often confounded under one letter in many languages. The difficulty of learning the values of the different letters is also much increased by the use of capitals and italics, many of which, especially the capitals, have entirely distinct forms. Compare A, a, *a,* G, g, &c. Besides being inadequate for the representation of the sounds of each individual language, the Roman alphabet has also lost to a great extent its universal and international character, the same letters being employed to signify totally distinct sounds in different languages. Compare *ch* in the English *church* with the French *chat,* the German *ach,* &c. Even in a single language one letter or letter-group often indicates a variety of distinct sounds. This is carried to such a pitch in English, that our alphabet really consists not of twenty-five letters (not including the divergent shapes of the capitals) but of more than two hundred letters and letter-groups, all of which have to be learnt separately.

With a rational alphabet like Visible Speech all this confusion is impossible; for the connection between each sound and its symbol is so intimate that the one can never be separated from the other, as in the Roman alphabet, where the association of sound and symbol is arbitrary and purely traditional. If Visible Speech were as perfect in its practical details as in its general theory, the only adequate solution of the question of spelling reform would evidently be to adopt it instead of the Roman alphabet. Unfortunately, however, Visible Speech is dependent on our knowledge of the formation of sounds, and until our knowledge is perfect, which it is as yet far from being, we have no guarantee that further discoveries may not oblige us to modify the details of our symbolisation. Until then Visible Speech must continue to be a purely scientific alphabet, which cannot be brought into general use till it is firmly based on a perfect and complete system of phonetic analysis, and has been tested thoroughly in practice.

The Roman alphabet, on the other hand, is quite independent of the scientific analysis of sounds. It has also been thoroughly tested in practice. Long experience and many experiments have selected the most legible and distinct types, and a script alphabet of the most practical character has been formed. In fact the difficulty of our present English spelling lies not so much in any of the inherent defects of the Roman alphabet as in our irrational use of it.

The immediate practical question of Spelling Reform resolves itself therefore into this—By what arrangement of the existing alphabet can the sounds of the English language be best represented?

The imperfections of the Roman alphabet may be remedied in various ways, but the fundamental consideration is whether to confine ourselves to the existing letters or to form new ones. The objections to the second alternative are evident. New types are costly; they disturb and complicate the existing founts; and there is often a difficulty in providing suitable script forms. If, on the other hand, we keep to the old types, we can reform our orthography without expense or disturbance of the existing machinery of the printing-offices, and what is of extreme importance, we are provided with a script alphabet of a thoroughly practical character. The practical experience of Mr. Ellis is important on this point. After expending much time and money in elaborating a new-type alphabet—the 'phonotypy' of Mr. Pitman—he has entirely abandoned the new-type principle as impracticable. He excludes even letters with accents and diacritics, which, being only cast for a few founts, act practically as new letters.

If then we exclude new letters as impracticable, we are obliged to fall back on digraphs, which are already largely employed in English and most other languages. The obvious objection to them is that they violate the natural principle of denoting every simple sound by a simple sign. In a rational alphabet such as Visible Speech, this principle is carried out consistently; the consonants of *she* and *the*, for instance, being denoted by single letters just as that of *see* is. But with the Roman alphabet, which does not claim to be rational and consistent, this principle cannot be carried out: our business is to make the best use of the materials we have, and if we can make a convenient and unambiguous symbol for a simple sound by joining two letters together, we are clearly right in doing so. In fact we may consider the *h* in *sh* and *th* simply as a diacritic written for convenience on a line with the letter it modifies. It would be possible to write and print the *h* above the *s* and *t*, or to make some kind of tag, but the expense of casting new types and the trouble of writing the new letters would not be repaid by any gain of ease or certainty in reading.

There is, however, one simple method of forming new letters without casting new types, which is often very convenient. This is by *turning* the letters, thus—ǝ, ɔ. These new letters are perfectly distinct in shape, and are easily written. The ǝ was first employed by Schmeller to denote the obscure *e*-sound in the German *gabe*, &c. Mr. Ellis, in his ' Palæotype,' uses it to denote the allied English sound in *but*.

A great improvement would be to do away with capitals entirely. They greatly add to the difficulty of learning the alphabet, have a disfiguring and incongruous effect among the lower-case letters, and serve no useful purpose whatever. Proper names are always recognised in speech by the context, and do not require to be marked in writing either, whose exclusive function is to give a faithful representation of the sounds of language. Whenever general distinctions are required, they can be indicated by the use of a larger or smaller fount, or by thick (Clarendon) or thin type.

We thus arrive at the general conclusion that a reformed alphabet must consist of the existing lower-case types, supplemented by digraphs, and, if necessary, by turned letters.

Employment of Letters.

This problem may also be stated thus—What values must be assigned to the letters that they may be most easily learnt, read, and written?   The obvious requisites are unambiguity and consistency, and that system which combines them in the highest degree (as far as the radical defects of the Roman alphabet will allow), while observing the practical considerations stated in the previous section, is the best.

It is clear that the defects of our present orthography are mainly due to its disregard of these fundamental principles.

Ambiguity is shown in the use of one symbol for several distinct sounds, as in *man, lane, ask, salt*, or of different symbols for one sound, as in *why, wine, eye, lie.* This fault is a violation of the fundamental principle of all rational spelling, viz. that of representing every sound by an invariable symbol (which may, however, be either a single letter or a digraph).

An alphabet is inconsistent when it fails to construct and apply its symbols on definite and uniform principles. It is, for instance, self-evident that a rational alphabet will indicate diphthongs by the juxtaposition of their elements, as in the *oi* of *oil,* which is really composed of *o* and *i.*   But in English this simple principle is not carried out with the other diphthongs.   In *out,* for instance, there is not a trace of an *o,* nor does its second element in the slightest degree resemble the *u* of *but.*   Again, *au,* which would be the proper symbol of the *ou* of *out,* does not denote a diphthong at all.

The practical effect of inconsistency is not only greatly to increase the number of arbitrary symbols, but also to make their acquisition more difficult, because of the conflicting associations of ideas thus engendered.

Before going any further it will be worth while to stop and consider what are the causes of the ambiguity, inconsistency and complexity of the present English spelling. When we have a definite idea of the cause, we shall be better able to devise a cure.

Up to the sixteenth century English spelling was mainly phonetic, like the present German. At that time the words *man, lane, care, father, water,* were all written with the same vowel because their vowels all had the same pronunciation, viz. that of the Italian *a* in *father.* Similarly *wine* was written with an *i* because its vowel really was the long sound of the *i* in *win, wine* being pronounced as *ween* is now, which last, again, had a pronunciation agreeing with its spelling. However, as literature developed, and the printing-press began to assert its authority, the spelling became more and more fixed, till at last it became entirely stationary, while the pronunciation went on changing without intermission, so that the *ee* of *ween* came to be the long sound of the *i* in *win*, while *wine* itself changed its long vowel into a diphthong, as in the present English. The *a* in *man*, &c. changed also in various ways without any corresponding change being made in the spelling. In short we may say that our present spelling does not represent the English we actually speak, but rather the language of the sixteenth century. In other words, the present confusion in our spelling is due to the abandonment of the

N

original Roman values of the letters, chiefly in the long vowels [a].

The only way of curing these evils is evidently to return to the original Roman values of the letters. If the beginner has once learnt to pronounce *a, e, i, o, u,* as in *glass, bet, bit, not, full,* he simply has to remember that long vowels are doubled, as in *biit*='beat,' and *fuul*='fool,' and diphthongs formed by the juxtaposition of their elements, as in *boi*='boy' and *hai*='high,' to be able to read at once the majority of the vowel symbols. Of the consonants, whose original values have been mostly preserved, little need be said at present.

Of course, the Roman alphabet requires to be supplemented, and this is a problem that requires much thought, in order to attain the maximum of consistency and simplicity, so that the new symbols may, if possible, suggest any relationship they may bear to other known ones. Thus æ as the symbol of the *a* in *man* at once suggests a sound intermediate between the true *a* in *father* and the *e* in *bet*, which the *a* in *man* really is. Further details must be reserved till we come to the analysis of the sounds of English, for, until we know what the elementary sounds really are, it is impossible to symbolise them intelligently.

Transition from and to the present Spelling.

We have hitherto considered the question of spelling reform solely from the point of view of those who learn

---

[a] For a general sketch of the changes of English pronunciation and spelling, see my ' History of English Sounds ' (Trübner).

to read for the first time. But we have also to consider the question of the transition from and to the present orthography. The two points of view may be contrasted thus :—

(1) Which system of spelling will be easiest learnt by a child learning to read for the first time?

(2) Which will come easiest to an adult who has already learnt on the received system?

The first of these two alternatives is, as we have seen, fully met by the simple principle of returning to the original Roman values of the letters. The second, on the other hand, requires that our new spelling should be based not on the original values of the letters but on some one of their present values. We may, then, distinguish two main classes of reformed spellings, (1) the Roman-value system, and (2) the English-value system. The only consistent and practical alphabet on the English-value system that has yet been produced is the 'Glossic' of Mr. Ellis.

Glossic is based on the principle of retaining the traditional means of expressing the sounds of English, but selecting one among the many symbols of each sound, and using it invariably to express that sound, rejecting, of course, all silent letters. Thus *ee* is taken as the sole representation of the sound of long *i*, being written not only in *feel*, but also in *reed, skeem,* = 'read' and 'scheme,' *peek* = 'pique,' &c. *ai* is written not only in *fail*, but also in *naim* = 'name,' *rain* = 'reign,' &c.

It cannot be denied that from its own point of view this system has considerable advantages. It would certainly cause the adults of the present generation less trouble than any Roman-value spelling, for any one who has learnt to read on the present system can read Glossic at sight. Mr. Ellis also thinks that those who had learnt Glossic would easily acquire the ordinary or 'Nomic' spelling, as he calls it. Before attempting to settle the relative merits of the Roman- and English-value systems, as regards ease of transition to and from the 'Nomic' spelling, it will be well to weigh the following considerations.

(1) In both systems a large number of words will retain their spellings entirely or almost unchanged. The following words, for instance, remain unchanged in both : *best, bend, desk, fed, let, men; if, hit, fish, wish, in, gift; on, hot, god, dog, pot; oil, boil, loin,* and many others.

(2) Many, indeed most of the remaining words, will undergo great alterations under both systems. Let us consider, for instance, that most of our written words are practically hieroglyphs, which we recognise individually by their consonant skeletons without thinking of the sounds they represent. Thus, if we substitute a (-) for the vowels in such words as *kn-ght, wr-ck, -n-gh,* we still recognise them without any difficulty, which would not be materially increased even by the introduction of different vowels. Now, on any system whatever of phonetic spelling, these words, which all contain silent consonants, entirely alter the shape of their skeletons, so that whether we write *nite, neit* or *nait, rec* or *rek, inuf* or *enəf,* the results are equally disguised to the eye, and can only be made out by an effort. Any possible superiority of one alphabet over another is thus very considerably reduced. To this may be added that, although in most cases where any superiority in point of resemblance to Nomic can be claimed by one system

over the other, the advantage is naturally on the side of Glossic, yet the Roman-value system often has the advantage on its side.   Thus the *u* in 'full,' 'pull,' 'put,' &c., and the *i* in 'pique,' 'machine,' 'marine,' &c., are preserved unchanged in the Roman-value system, while in Glossic *u* being used to represent the vowel in 'but' cannot be retained in 'full,' and the *i* of 'pique,' &c. must of course be written *ee*.

(3) Again, the very resemblance of Glossic to Nomic often causes very puzzling confusions.   Thus 'latter,' 'ridding, 'supper,' become *later, riding, super*, while the Nomic 'later,' 'riding,' 'super(fine),' are represented by *laiter, reiding, seuperfein*.   The Roman-value system, being more remote from Nomic, is much less liable to such cross-associations.   In fact, the relation of Glossic to Nomic is very like that of two closely allied languages, such as Danish and Swedish, or Spanish and Portuguese. Although Danes and Swedes soon learn to understand one another's languages, they hardly ever, even after years of study, succeed in speaking each other's languages with real accuracy, the very nearness of the two languages, with their constant deviations from one another in matters of detail, causing constant confusion and cross-association.

THE REPRESENTATION OF SOUNDS.

Vowels.

Vowels are formed by retraction of the *back* of the tongue, as in 'father'; by advancing the *front* of the tongue, as in 'b*i*t'; or else they are *mixed*, as in 'b*i*rd,' in which the tongue is in a position half-way between back and front. By height they are *high*, as in 'h*i*t,' *mid*, as in 'h*a*te, or *low*, as in 'h*a*t. The vowels of these three words are all front, but the distinctions of height apply to back and mixed vowels as well. Thus the *u* of 'full' is high-back, just as that of 'hit' is high front. All these vowels may be further modified by labialization, or *rounding*. Thus, if the *ee* of 'feel' is pronounced with narrowed lip-opening, we obtain the French *u* in 'lune'—the high-front-round. There are besides other modifications caused by the shape of the tongue itself.

Of the large number of possible vowels only a small proportion is employed in each language.

Again, among the special vowels of any one language we must distinguish between those differences which are *distinctive*, that is, to which differences of meaning correspond, and those which are not. Thus the first elements of the diphthongs in 'by' and 'out' vary considerably: some people sound them broad as in 'f*a*ther,' some thin, as in 'm*a*n,' with various intermediate sounds. And yet the meaning of the words remains unchanged. The distinction between the vowels of 'men' and 'man,' on the other hand, though really slighter than that of the different pronunciations of 'by' and 'out,' is a distinctive one.

It often happens that two sounds, though formed in different ways, have nearly the same effect on the ear. Thus the English vowel in 't*u*rn' is formed in a totally different way from the French one in 'p*eu*r, the former being an unrounded, the latter a rounded vowel, and yet they are hardly distinguishable by an untrained ear.

The consequence is that two such vowels are never employed together in the same language to distinguish the meanings of words, and for practical purposes they may be considered as variations of the same vowel. Hence we have to distinguish not so much between *sounds* as between *groups of sounds.* One of the most important distinctions of these groups is that of close and 'open,' the open vowels being generally formed by a 'low' position of the tongue or by some other widening of the mouth passage.

Disregarding special exceptions in individual languages, we may assume the following as the chief distinctive groups in language generally:

A. Unrounded.

(1) the dull-back,   b*u*t.
(2) the clear-back,   f*a*ther.
(3) the mixed [a],   t*u*rn, fath*e*r, gab*e* (German).
(4) the high-front,   b*i*t, b*ea*t.
(5) the close-front,   *été* (French).
(6) the open-front,   m*e*n, m*a*re, m*a*n.

B. Rounded.

(7) high-back,   f*u*ll, f*oo*l.
(8) close-back,   s*o* (German).
(9) open-back,   f*o*lly, f*a*ll.
(10) high-front,   l*u*ne (French).
(11) close-front,   p*eu* (French).
(12) open-front,   p*eu*r (French).

[a] The vowel in 'turn' is open-mixed, that in 'gabe' close-mixed.

Of these groups the mixed (3) is, as remarked above almost identical in sound with the close and open front (11, 12), with which latter the dull-back (1) is often identified, although in sound it is really intermediate between them and the clear-back (2). In practice, therefore, the symbols for 11 and 12 will also suffice for 1 and 3.

a, i and *u*, at once supply symbols for 2, 4 and 7 respectively. For 10 we have only to restore *y* to its original Roman value, which it still retains in Danish and Swedish. If we assign *e* to the close-front (5) and *o* to the close-back-round (8), in accordance with the general European tradition, we must find letters for the corresponding open vowels. For the open-front (6) æ at once suggests itself, the *a* indicating openness. For the open *o* (9) there is no type ready to hand; I propose therefore to adopt the turned ɔ used by Mr. Ellis in his Palæotype. This letter, which is really a turned *c*, is meant to suggest a turned *o*, which is impracticable. For the rounded *e* (11) the turned ə may be used, and for the open sound (12) œ. We thus obtain the perfectly parallel forms *i, e,* æ, and *y,* ə, œ. The last two at the same time supply symbols for the special English *u* in 'but' (1) and 'turn' (3).

Diphthongs are, of course, symbolised by the juxtaposition of their elements. The following are the English diphthongs :—

ai	*as in*	a*i*sle.
au	,,	n*ow*.
oi	,,	b*oi*l.
ei	,,	v*ei*l.
ou	,,	s*ou*l.

Diphthongs in all languages vary greatly in their constituents, and the above combinations must be understood as simply denoting general tendencies. Thus *ai* does not literally imply a combination of the *a* in 'father' and the *i* in 'bit,' but merely a movement in that direction. We may start, not with a full-back vowel, but with a mixed one, which may move towards *i*, but without reaching it in fact the commonest pronunciation of 'aisle' may be represented by *əel.* In the same way *ei* only implies a front vowel moving upwards, and, as a matter of fact, the starting-point may be either close or open *e* or even the *a* of 'man.' Indeed *ei* often begins with a mixed vowel, in which case 'veil' is confounded with 'vile.'

Note that *ei* and *ou* in English supply the place of close long *ee* and *oo*, which most English people are unable to pronounce.

ii and *uu* are often diphthongised in a peculiar way in English, by being made to end in the consonants *y* and *w* respectively, *wiin* (ween) and *fuul* (fool) becoming *wiyn* and *fuwl*.

Having thus laid a general foundation, we may proceed to discuss some special modifications required in English.

As there is no short close *e* or *o* in English, it is superfluous to use *æ* and *ɔ* to denote the quality of sounds whose openness is always implied by their shortness. We can, therefore, discard *ɔ* altogether in English, and employ *æ* to denote the peculiar *a* in 'man,' for which it would otherwise be difficult to find an appropriate letter.

The longs of *æ* and *ɔ* may be expressed, as with the other vowels, by doubling—*ææ, ɔɔ*. But as this is inconvenient, and as *ɔ* is not used in English, it is better to denote the long of *æ* by *ae*, the separation of the letters

implying length.   Long ɔ may, on this analogy, be denoted by *ao*.

R AND ITS MODIFICATIONS.

The consonant *r* in English only occurs before a vowel,
either in the same or the next word, as in 'erring'
(eriq), 'far off' (faar aof).   When not followed by a
vowel, that is, either by a pause or a consonant, it is
weakened into ə—the *er* of 'father.'   After *aa* and *əə* the
ə is absorbed, as in 'bar' (baa), 'farther' (faadhə), 'her'
(hoe), 'heard' (hoed), the first two being indistinguishable
from 'baa' and 'father.'   ə is sometimes dropped after
ao, especially before a consonant, as in 'floor,' 'floored,'
although the full *flaoə, flaoəd* are most usual in careful
speech, especially when the ə is final.   After other vowels
ə is preserved throughout, also when the *r* is sounded as
a full consonant: compare 'air' (aeə), aired' (aeəd), and
 airy' (aeəri) with 'far off' (faar aof), 'her own' (hoer
oun), and 'flooring' (flaoriq).

The following table will give a general idea of these
changes:—

faar aof (far off)	faa	faadhə (farther).
hoer oun (her own)	hoe	hoed (heard).
fiiəriq (fearing)	fiiə	fiiəd (feared).
aeəriq (airing)	aeə	aeəd (aired).
muuəriq (mooring)	muuə	muuəd (moored).
flaoriq (flooring)	flaoə	flaoəd (floored).
faiəriq (firing)	faiə	faiəd (fired).
flauəri (flowery, floury)	flauə	flauəd (flowered).
leiəriq (layering)	leiə	leiəd (layered).
louəriq (lowering)	louə	louəd (lowered).

Note that *eiǝ(r)* and *ouǝ(r)* in rapid, especially in vulgar speech, often pass into *aeǝ(r)* and *aoǝ(r)*.

When *r* is preceded by a short vowel, as in 'hurry' (hǝri), merry' (meri), no *ǝ* is generated.

Unaccented Vowels.

The two chief unaccented vowels in English are *ǝ* and *i*, together with the rarer *o*. The former may be regarded as a shortened *oe*, as in ' her,' into which it always passes when emphasised or prolonged, but it is really nothing but a voice murmur without any definite configuration. The *i* is an intermediate vowel between *i* and *e*, and might as well be written *e* as *i*. It may be regarded either as a very open *i* or a very close *e*.

The following are examples of *ǝ* :—

ǝtemt (attempt), ǝpouz (oppose), ǝpon (upon), tǝdei (to-day).

soufǝ (sofa), menshǝn (mention), peishǝns (patience), kærǝt (carrot).

faadhǝ (father), onǝ (honour), mezhǝ (measure).

faowǝd (forward), shepǝd (shepherd).

feivǝrit (favourite), mezhǝriq (measuring).

ǝ is often dropped before *l*, *n*, and *m*; always when the *ǝ* is preceded by *t* or *d* and followed by *l* or *n* :—

metl (metal), gaadn (garden), gaadniq (gardening), mǝtn (mutton).

iivl (evil), loukl (local), simbl (cymbal, symbol).

When two or more unaccented *ǝ*s or *i*s follow one another, one of them is often thrown out, as in—

hist(ə)ri (history), feiv(ə)rit (favourite), vedzh$\left\{ {ə \atop i} \right\}$təbl (vegetable).

i is less common than *ə*   It is most usual as a weakening of front vowels, especially when *i* or *y* is written :—

piti (pity), məndi (Monday)
divaid (divide), ditekt (detect).
ræbit (rabbit), fishiz (fishes), əbiliti (ability).

It is the regular unaccented vowel before *dzh*, even when *a* is written:—

vilidzh (village), kæridzh (carriage), kolidzh (college).

In rapid speech *i* is apt to pass into *ə*, except when final.

Unaccented *o* in ordinary speech is simply *ə* rounded. When dwelt on it becomes *ou*.   Examples are—

pəteito (potato), folo (follow), felo (fellow).

In rapid speech this *o* passes into *ə*.

These vowels occur also in unaccented monosyllables. Compare 'a man' (ə mæn) with 'against' (əgenst), 'to go' (tə gou) with 'to-day' (tə dei), 'for all' (fər aol) with 'forgive' (fəgiv), 'of course' (əv kaoəs) with 'offence' (əfens).

the and *to* have two distinct unaccented forms.   Before consonants they both have *ə*, while before vowels they assume the fuller forms *dhi* and *tu*:—

dhə mæn (the man), dhi enəmi (the enemy).
tə gou (to go), tu entə (to enter).

It was, I believe, first noticed by Mr. Ellis that 'that' as a demonstrative is always full *dhæt*, while as a conjunction and relative pronoun it becomes *dhət*:—ai nou

dhət dhæt dhət dhæt mæn sez iz truu (I know that that
that that man says is true).

Consonants.

As regards the use of the letters there can be no question about the values of the following :—b, d, f, g, h, k, l,
m, n, p, r, s, t, v, w, z.

This leaves *c, j, q, x* undisposed of. We also have *y*,
which is not required as a vowel-symbol in English. If
we allow *y* to retain its present value, we can also retain *j*
as a convenient abbreviation of *dzh*. For *tsh* we have *ch*,
which, by the omission of the superfluous *h*, can be reduced to simple *c*. We thus have *c* and *j* perfectly parallel.
q may very well be taken to represent the back nasal *ng*,
as Mr. Ellis has done in his Palæotype. *x* lastly, if employed at all, must in consistency be extended to all *ks* s
in the language, not only in such words as *six*, but also
in *rex* (wrecks), *cex* (cheques), &c.

These contractions fully counterbalance the necessity
of retaining the digraphs *th* and *sh*, to which must of
course be added *dh* and *zh*. *wh* is very generally made
into *w* in Southern English, but it is well to keep up the
distinction on the chance of its being afterwards revived.
The breath *yh* (= German 'ich') sometimes occurs in such
words as 'hue' (yhuu), more commonly, however, pronounced *hyuu*, with a separate *h* before the *y*.

Consonants are often dropped in English. Thus the *h*
of the personal pronouns is generally dropped when they
come after a verb, and are unaccented, as in *ai sao im* (I
saw him). *Saw her* and *soar* are both pronounced *saoə*.
The *d* of *and* is generally dropped before a consonant, as

in *cət n cəm əgen* (cut and come again), where the vowel
is dropped also on account of the *t* and *n* (p. 187 above).

Assimilations also occur in rapid speech.   Thus, many
people who pronounce the *q* of 'going,' &c. quite distinctly in most cases, regularly change the back into the
point nasal (n), when it is followed by a point consonant
(t, d, n), as in *gouin tə . . .* (going to . . .).   In *I can't go*
the *t* is generally dropped, and the point nasal is often
assimilated to the *g* by being made into the back nasal *q*
—*ai kaaq gou.*

A<small>CCENT AND</small> Q<small>UANTITY</small>.

The chief accent or stress in each word may be marked
by (·) following the letter on which the accent begins :—
əg·enst (against), *fəg·iv* (forgive).   To indicate the secondary
accent, when necessary, (:) may be used :—*i:nkənv·iinyəns*
(inconvenience), *dist:rəktəb·iliti* (destructibility).   These
very convenient marks were introduced by Mr. Ellis.   In
practice the accent need only be marked when it is on
some other than the first syllable.   Thus it need not be
marked in *foutogræf* (photograph).

Unaccented vowels are always shortened.   Thus *hii* in
hii gouz (he goes) is much shorter than in *it iz hii* (ıt is
he), but its vowel is quite distinct from the regular short *i*
in 'hit.'   As this shortening is always implied by the want
of accent, it need not be marked : *hi gouz* would imply
that the *i* was pronounced as in 'hit.'

Emphasis, or the accent of a word in a sentence as
distinguished from that of a syllable in a word, is marked
by a (·) before the word.   Such subordinate monosyllables
as 'he,' 'she,' 'it,' 'and,' 'if,' 'to,' 'for,' &c., are assumed

to be unaccented unless thus marked. We thus distinguish between *hii gouz* and *it iz ·hii*, between *hii hæz mai buk* (he has my book) and *it iz ·mai buk not ·hiz* (it is *my* book, not *his*). Principal words, such as nouns, non-auxiliary verbs and adjectives, which regularly receive a full accent, may be marked in the same way whenever they are made exceptionally emphatic, thus *ai ·fəg·iv yu* indicates that the second syllable of *fəg·iv* is uttered with extra emphasis.

List of English Symbols.

The following table gives a complete list of the English vowel symbols in the 'Romic' system I propose, together with those consonant ones which require elucidation, with examples.

A. *Vowels.*

aa : pap*a*, f*ar*, gl*a*ss, *a*fter, *au*nt. [Before *s* and *f* or before two (pronounced) consonants *aa* is sometimes shortened, and sometimes becomes *æ* : *glæs, ænt.*]

æ : m*a*n.

ae : *ae*rate, b*ea*r, f*a*re. [Always followed by *ə*.]

ai : Isa*i*ah, *ai*sle, w*i*ne.

ao : extr*a*ordinary, br*oa*d, m*o*re.

au : F*au*st, n*ow*, n*ou*n.

e : r*e*d.

ei : th*ey*, v*ei*l, n*a*me.

i : *i*ll, fish*e*s.

ii, iy : mach*i*ne, f*ee*l.

o : n*o*t, cl*o*th, cr*o*ss, s*o*ft. [Often becomes *ao* before *th*, *s*, and *f* : *klaoth, kraos, saoft.*]

oi : b*oy*, b*oi*l.
ou : fl*ow*, s*ou*l, st*o*ne.
u : f*u*ll, p*u*t, g*oo*d.
uu, *uw* : tr*u*th, r*ue*, f*oo*l.
ə : *u*p, c*o*me; fath*er*, h*ere*.
oe : h*er*, t*ur*n, h*ear*d.

B. *Consonants.*

c : *ch*ur*ch*, ca*tch*.
dh : *th*en, wi*th*.
j : *j*u*dg*e, *g*entle.
q : si*ng*, fi*ng*er.
sh : fi*sh*.
th : *th*ink.
x : si*x*, wre*cks*.
y : *y*oung.
zh : rou*g*e, plea*s*ure.

NEW TYPES.

Although new types should be avoided at first, their exclusion is only a practical consideration, not a matter of principle, and there is no reason why they should not afterwards be introduced by degrees. Thus Mr. Pitman's ŋ is unquestionably superior to *q* as a symbol of the back nasal *ng*, for its shape at once associates it with the other nasals *n*, *m*. Again the Greek θ and δ (or perhaps better the Anglo-Saxon ƀ) would do very well for *th* and *dh*, both being easily written. The long *s* and tailed *z* of Pitman's Phonotypy are also excellent letters for *sh* and *zh*. We should thus avoid the ambiguity of such words as *pothuk* (pothook), which at present can only be avoided by writing *pot-huk*.

SPECIAL CONSIDERATIONS.

VARIETIES OF PRONUNCIATION.

It is clear that as soon as spelling ceases to adapt itself to existing varieties of pronunciation—whether 'colloquialisms,' 'vulgarisms,' or 'provincialisms'—it ceases to be phonetic.

Spelling apart from the sounds it represents has, properly speaking, no meaning, no existence whatever. A picture of a man at once suggests the idea 'man' to any one, and the sounds represented by the letter-group *man* suggest the same idea to all English-speaking people, but the letters *m, a, n* only suggest sounds, not ideas. After a time, of course, we learn to associate ideas with letter-groups without thinking of the sounds, but this is necessarily a secondary process, although it may be carried so far that the connection between the letters and their sounds becomes to a great extent forgotten—till, in short, the spelling becomes *unphonetic*, as in the present English. The only way to cure these evils—which is the object of all spelling reform—is to restore spelling to its only legitimate function, that of symbolising sounds.

It follows necessarily that if two people have different pronunciations, their spellings must also be different. If A, who pronounces *glæs* (glass), *gæl* (girl), *iidhə* (either), is to be compelled to write *glaas, goel, aidhə* because B pronounces so, phonetic spelling becomes a mere mockery, and is really no more phonetic than the present system, which writes *knight* and *wright* because people pronounced so three hundred years ago, although half of the letters are absolutely unmeaning now.

As a matter of fact, these differences, which hardly ever cause the slightest difficulty even in the most rapid speech, and, indeed, generally pass quite unheeded, cannot possibly cause any difficulty to the reader, who has time to consider deliberately the meaning of any passage, if necessary. When divergences of pronunciation increase to such a degree as to make a faithful phonetic representation of them unintelligible, or nearly so, to those acquainted only with the standard form of speech, it is certain that the spoken pronunciation itself will prove still more difficult.

In fact, one of the worst features of a fixed orthography is that it loses all control of pronunciation, and thus indirectly proves the cause of such changes as have completely changed the character of English in the last few centuries. If those careless speakers of the seventeenth century who used to drop the initial consonants in such words as *write* and *know* had been obliged to omit them in writing as well as in speech, it is probable that the change would have been nipped in the bud, and people would have seen that uniformity of spelling is a delusion, unless based on a corresponding uniformity of pronunciation.

The history of *h* and *r* in modern times is an instructive instance of how pronunciation may be controlled by a changing spelling. It is certain that if English had been left to itself the sound *h* would have been as completely lost in the standard language as it has been in most of the dialects. But the distinction between *house* and *'ouse*, although in itself a comparatively slight one, being easily marked in writing, such spellings as *'ouse* came to be used in novels, &c. as an easy way of suggesting a vulgar speaker. The result was to produce a purely artificial reaction against the natural tendency to drop the *h*, its retention being now considered an almost infallible test of education and refinement. The weakening of *r* into a vowel, and its absorption into the vowel that precedes it, although really quite as injurious to the force and intelligibility of the language as the dropping of *h*, not being easily marked in writing, passes unheeded, and, indeed, few people realise the fact that they make no difference whatever between such words as *father* and *farther*. Indeed, if such a reformed spelling as Glossic is adopted, in which these artificial distinctions are still kept up, there is no reason why in the next half century *r* may not utterly disappear everywhere except initially; *hear*, for instance, becoming identical in sound with *he*.

If the high literary cultivation of the seventeenth and eighteenth centuries, and the consequent fixity of the orthography, not only failed to prevent, but positively encouraged the most sweeping changes in pronunciation, it is certain that the same effects will produce the same causes in the future. No one who has paid any attention to the tendencies of English pronunciation will deny that the following hypothetical changes of pronunciation in the next fifty or sixty years are all possible and some of them extremely probable (the pronunciations are given in the received spelling) :—

been	*becomes*	bane.
bane	,,	bine.
bine	,,	barn.
boon	,,	been (*through* bün).

Indeed, many of these changes are already in progress.
I have myself heard *take time* pronounced in a way which
made it sound not very unlike *tike tarm*, and this from
speakers who, although not very refined, certainly belonged
to the upper middle class.

The result of these and similar changes will be that in
another century any fixed scheme of reform adopted now
will be nearly as unphonetic as our present Nomic spelling.   It must also be remembered that by that time
England, America, and Australia will be speaking mu-
tually unintelligible languages, owing to their independent
changes of pronunciation.

The only way to meet these evils is strictly to subordinate spelling to pronunciation.   One very important
result of this will be that instead of teaching spelling we
shall have to teach pronunciation.   Our maxim will be,
'Take care of the pronunciation, and the spelling will
take care of itself.'   If it is wrong to confound *father*
and *farther* in spelling, it must be still more wrong to
confound them in pronunciation.   Then the question of
restoring the consonantal pronunciation of *r* throughout
will perhaps arise—certainly that of arresting further
change will.   School-inspectors will examine not in spelling but in pronunciation, elocution, and intelligent reading—subjects which are now absolutely ignored as branches
of general education.   When a firm control of pronunciation
has thus been acquired, provincialisms and vulgarisms will
at last be entirely eliminated, and one of the most important barriers between the different classes of society will
thus be abolished.

It must, however, be remembered that these results are
not to be attained by the adoption of any system indif-

ferently that may be proposed. What is wanted is a simple, consistent, and above all *elastic* spelling, which, within certain practical limits, will adapt itself to every change of pronunciation. Changes of pronunciation cannot be controlled by any spelling based on the Nomic values of the letters. There is, for instance, no reason why *oo* should represent the sound of long *u* any more than that of long *i*, nor consequently why the *uu* of 'boon' should not change through *byyn* (with the French *u*) into *biin* without any change of spelling being thought necessary, and consequently without any control of such possible changes being exercised.

International Intelligibility.

One very important result of a return to the Roman values of the letters would be the restoration of the original harmony of the English with the Continental values of the letters, which would much facilitate the acquisition of English by foreigners, and vice versa. At present, English people and foreigners have to learn each other's languages almost entirely by eye, unless thoroughly taught by a native, and consequently are utterly at a loss when brought face to face with the spoken language—in fact, they have to learn the same language twice over. Thus when a German sees the English written word *right* he easily associates it with his own *recht*, as also the English *name* with the German *name*, but when he hears the genuine *rait* and *neim*, he is thrown completely off the scent. Conversely, when an Englishman comes across the German *knie* for the first time, he at once thinks of his own *knee*, and naturally drops the *k* in the German word as well as in the English : if he were used to see the English word spelt *nii*, he would never think of dropping the *k* in German.

It will, of course, be urged by the advocates of historical spelling that the silent letters in *right* and *knee* are really valuable helps in acquiring the language. All this really amounts to is, that sixteenth-century English bears a much closer resemblance to German than nineteenth-century English does, consequently that a German will learn the former more easily than the latter, and that an Englishman who knows sixteenth-century English will thereby learn German more easily. The practical result is, of course, that English has to be learnt twice over both by the English themselves and by foreigners. The worst of it is, that instead of learning the older stage of our language on an intelligent and systematic plan, we have it forced on us—whether we really want it or not—in the shape of a garbled and imperfect orthography, which, instead of giving us clear ideas of the language of the period it represents, only serves to hopelessly confuse our notions of our present language.

Of course the orthographies of most of the Continental languages require reform as well as English ; French, especially, most urgently demands a thorough change. Indeed, there is no reason why foreigners should not learn French on a phonetic system, leaving the present French spelling to be acquired afterwards, even if the French themselves do not inaugurate a reform.

There are many significant facts in the pronunciation and spelling of English which show that the return to the Roman values of the vowels would not be by any means so violent a change as is generally supposed. Even without going beyond the commonest words in our vocabulary we have whole classes of words like *machine, marine, oblique, antique,* &c., in which long *i* retains its Roman value. In geographical names, such as *Alabama, Chicago, Granada, Medina, Messina,* the accented vowels all have the Roman values. In such names as *Isaiah, Achaia, Cairo,* the diphthong also has its strict analytical value. Indeed, the tendency is becoming stronger and stronger to retain as much as possible the native pronunciation of foreign names. The definite adoption of the Romic principle by the Indian government, and the reformed pronunciation of Latin, are all most important moves in the same direction.

History and Etymology.

One of the commonest arguments against phonetic spelling is that it would destroy the historical and etymological value of the present system. One writer protests against it as a 'reckless wiping out of the whole history of the language,' imagining, it appears, that as soon as a phonetic alphabet has once firmly established itself, the existing Nomic literature will at once disappear by magic, together with all the older documents of the language from Alfred to Chaucer. It need hardly be said that a few months' study of the language of Chaucer, or, better still, of the Anglo-Saxon Gospels, or, best of all, of both of them, would give what a life spent in the mechanical employment of our Nomic orthography fails to give, namely, some of the materials on which a rudimentary knowledge of the history and etymology of the English language might be based.

As a matter of fact, our present spelling is in many particulars a far from trustworthy guide in etymology, and often, indeed, entirely falsifies history. Such spellings as *island, author, delight, sovereign,* require only to be mentioned. and there are hundreds of others involving equally gross blunders, many of which have actually corrupted the spoken language!

Even if we carried out—that is, if it were possible— the principle of etymological spelling consistently, by writing each word in its primitive Indo-Germanic form, writing, for instance, *klaipawardha* for *lord,* we should only be giving a portion of the materials of etymology. We should have to give in brackets or foot-notes to each word the Anglo-Saxon and Middle-English, together with the present English forms, the last *in phonetic spelling,* and, lastly, a brief abstract of the laws which govern the various changes of form and meaning. Even if we arbitrarily resolve not to trace our history further back than the sixteenth century we shall have to write each word twice over. It is absurd to say that the spelling *knight,* for instance, throws light on any word in the present English. Of course, the word meant is *nait.* But where do we find the existence of such a word even hinted at? All that the spelling *knight* tells us is that a word existed in a certain form in sixteenth-century English: it tells us nothing about its present form.

In short, historical spelling *destroys the materials on which alone history itself can be based.* This is the case in the English of the last few centuries. The word 'name,' as its spelling indicates, was in Chaucer's time pronounced *naamə,* or something like it. It is now *neim,* although still written 'name.' Now there must clearly have been several intermediate stages between *naamǝ* and *neim*—the one word certainly did not change straight into the other. If these changes had taken place in the period before Chaucer, we should have been able to trace their progress step by step in the changes of the spelling, which, as it is, not only fails to record these changes, but gives the false impression that the English language, in this word at least, has remained unchanged since the time of Chaucer. Hence the actual history of the English language since the invention of printing has to be investigated in a most laborious and uncertain way, quite independently of its written form, so far as the sounds are concerned. The investigations of Mr. Ellis have proved that 'name' passed through the following stages: *naamǝ, naam, næǣm* (long of *æ* in 'man'), *naem, neem, neim*. It is clear that if a consistent and etymological spelling had become fixed in the Indo-Germanic languages, there would have been no Grimm's law, no etymology, in short no philology at all possible.

The idea, too, that because etymology is an amusing and instructive pursuit, it should therefore be dragged into practical orthography, is about as reasonable as it would be to insist on every one having Macaulay's History of England permanently chained round his neck, because history is an improving study.

In conclusion, it may be observed that it is mainly among the class of half-taught dabblers in philology that etymological spelling has found its supporters. All true philologists and philological bodies have uniformly denounced it as a monstrous absurdity both from a practical and a scientific point of view.

DETAILED COMPARISON OF GLOSSIC AND ROMIC.

The elementary vowel symbols of Glossic are contained in the following key-words:

gn*a*t, b*aa*, b*ai*t, c*au*l.

n*e*t, b*ee*t, h*ei*ght, f*eu*d.

kn*i*t.

n*o*t, c*oo*l, c*oa*l, f*oi*l, f*ou*l.

n*u*t, f*uo*t (for *foot*).

The only consonants that require notice (reserving *r* for the present) are :

*ch*est, *j*est.

*th*in, *dh*en (for *then*) ; ru*sh*, rou*zh*e (for *rouge*).

Glossic is an attempt to form a phonetic system of writing based on the present values of the letters. It is, therefore, necessarily a compromise. As Mr. Ellis himself remarks, 'Combinations rather than separate letters have definite sounds. Thus *u* in *nut* has one sound, but the combinations *uo, ou, eu*, have no trace of this sound.' Of course, when the learner has once acquired these combinations he is taught to apply them consistently. In fact Glossic depends mainly on the *phonetic use of a limited number of unphonetic combinations* (that is, combinations whose pronunciation does not depend on that of their elements). In Romic, on the other hand, the combinations (diphthongs, &c.) are as phonetic as the actual words themselves, so that the learner of Romic only has to learn the values of six

simple vowel-symbols, whereas the learner of Glossic
has to master more than twenty, which are not only
totally disconnected and arbitrary, but also suggest all
kinds of puzzling cross-associations. Of course, even
this is an enormous improvement on Nomic, in which
there are more than two hundred combinations, many
of which are employed almost at random.

The weakest part of Glossic is its treatment of *r*.
r in Glossic is used both for the consonant and for the
vocalised *r* (=ə), as in *peer* (piiə), and hence must be
doubled in *peerring* (=piiəriq), the first *r* indicating the
ə, the second the true *r*. əə in 'err,' 'burn,' &c., is
written *er*: *er*='err,' *bern*='burn.' Hence *deterring*=
Romic *dit·oeriq*, on the analogy of *peerring*. But *er* before
a vowel has the totally distinct value of Romic *er*, as in
the word *ering*='erring' (eriq).

Again, the conventional *ar* and *or* are retained to
represent the same sounds as *aa* and *au*, *faadher* and
fardher, for instance, being kept distinct, although their
pronunciation is identical.

Here the phonetic character of Glossic entirely breaks
down, for such distinctions as those last mentioned can
only be taught by spelling lessons. This is equally the
case with such spellings as those of the final vowels in
faadher and *soafa* ('sofa'), where the same sound is
represented in two distinct ways. Before the learner
can decide whether to write *soafa* or *soafer*, he must
stop and consider whether a following vowel would bring
out the *r* or not.

These considerations show clearly at what a sacrifice
of the most essential principles of phonetic writing Glossic
retains its similarity to the existing spelling. Any attempt

to make the writing of *r* phonetic could only produce such spellings as these, which would quite defeat the aims of the system :—*peeu* (=peer), *peeuring* (peering), *sauu* (soar), *faadha, faadhu* (farther), *soafer* (sofa), *ergenst, ugenst* (against), &c.

In short, Glossic cannot be regarded as a consistently phonetic system even on its own principle of taking the values of combinations for granted.

The following tables have been prepared with a view to enable the reader to judge for himself on the relations of Glossic and Romic to one another and to Nomic. They consist of typical words chosen impartially to represent most of the more important values of the different Nomic letters and combinations, together with the Glossic and Romic spellings.

A. VOWELS.

Nomic.	Glossic.	Romic.	Nomic.	Glossic.	Romic.
man	man	mæn	thief	theef	thiif
lane	lain	lein	lie	lei	lai
hare	hair	haeər			
ask	aask	aask	on	on	on
wall	waul	waol	hole	hoal	houl
salt	solt	solt	none	nun	nən
			more	moar	maoɔr
nail	nail	neil	word	werd	woed
air	air	aeər	no	noa	nou
			do	doo	duu
saw	sau	sao			
			soon	soon	suun
ten	ten	ten	good	guod	gud
he	hee	hii	blood	blud	bləd
where	whair	whaeər	door	doar	daoər
stern	stern	stoen			
			oath	oath	outh
see	see	sii	oar	oar	aoər
sea	see	sii	woe	woa	wou
bear	bair	baeər	shoe	shoo	shuu
earth	erth	oeth			
head	hed	hed	oil	oil	oil
break	braik	breik	boy	boi	boi
veil	vail	veil	out	out	aut
key	kee	kii	soul	soal	soul
eye	ei	ai	you	yoo	yuu
			four	foar	faoer
few	feu	fyuu			
grew	groo	gruu	up	up	əp
			tune	teun	tyuun
in	in	in	rule	rool	ruul
myth	mith	mith	burst	berst	boest
wine	wein	wain	full	fuol	ful
first	ferst	foest			
pique	peek	piik			

B. DROPPED CONSONANTS.

Nomic.	Glossic.	Romic.	Nomic.	Glossic.	Romic.
debt lamb	det lam	det læm	hymn	him	him
scene	seen	siin	psalm	saam	saam
schism	sizm	sizm	phthisis	tizis	tizis
gnaw reign	nau rain	nao rein	isle	eil	ail

C. VARYING CONSONANTS.

Nomic.	Glossic.	Romic.	Nomic.	Glossic.	Romic.
cat cease ocean	kat sees oashen	kæt siis oushən	see as sugar	see az shuoger	sii æz shugər
chin scheme	chin skeem	cin skiim	thick this Thames	thik dhis Temz	thik dhis temz
get George	get Joarj	get jaoj	vex	veks	vex
ghost laugh through	goast laaf throo	goust laaf thruu	example Xerxes	egzaampl Zerkseez	egzaampl zoexiiz

The results of a detailed study of this table may be conveniently, though somewhat roughly, summed up in the following lists, in which, however, only the commonest groups are given, each represented by its typical word :—

I. *Unchanged in both.*	II. *Changed in both.*	III. *Unchanged in Glossic.*	IV. *Unchanged in Romic.*
(5)	(12)	(11)	(5)
ask ᵃ	lane	man	veil
ten	hare	nail	pique
in	wall	saw	soul
on	salt	(air)	full
oil	sea	(stern)	rule
	bear	see	
	head	few	
	wine	soon	
	hole	oath	
	none	out	
	good	up	
	blood		

We see that out of a total of thirty-three typical words more than a half either remain unchanged or else undergo equally violent changes *under any possible scheme of reform.* Also that only a third of the whole thirty-three remain unchanged in Glossic, from which the two in parentheses ought, strictly speaking, to be excluded, as their agreement with Nomic is obtained at a great sacrifice of phonetic consistency.

The results are, of course, rough. Mathematical accuracy would require that the number of words belonging to each group should be counted, and the relative

---

ᵃ May be considered as practically unchanged.

importance and frequency of each word ascertained, all of which would be a very laborious work.

It is, however, clear that the ease with which Glossic is read by those familiar with Nomic is not inconsistent with considerable divergences between the two. It is, therefore, an important question to consider what would be the effect of the greater divergence between Nomic and Romic on the first attempts of a Nomic reader to understand Romic. If the difference between Glossic and Romic in ease of acquirement by a Nomic reader amount, as it is possible it may, only to half-an-hour's preliminary study of the elementary symbols of the latter, and the principles of their combination, then it is a serious question whether it is worth while sacrificing the interests of future generations of learners to the half-hours of the comparatively few who have to make the transition from Nomic to Romic.

SPECIMENS.

A. Uncontracted.

(Writing *tsh*, *dzh* in full and retaining *ng*.)

I.

huusoue·və hiiərith dhiiz seiingz əv main, ənd duuith dhəm, ai wil laikn him ənt·uu ə waiz mæn, whitsh bilt hiz haus əp·on ə rok : ənd dhə rein dis·endid, ənd dhə flədz keim, ənd dhə windz bluu, ənd biit əp·on dhæt haus; ənd it fel not : fər it wəz faundid əp·on ə rok.

ənd evriwən dhət hiirith dhiiz seiingz əv main, ənd duuith dhəm not, shæl bii laikənd ənt·uu ə fuulish mæn, whitsh bilt hiz haus əp·on dhə sænd : ənd dhə rein dis·endid, ənd dhə flədz keim, ənd dhə windz bluu, ənd biit əp·on dhæt haus; ənd it fel : ənd greit wəz dhə faol əv it.

B. Contracted.

(*c* = *tsh*, *j* = *dzh*, *q* = *ng*.   *a* for *aa*, the length being implied.   The combinations *iiə*, &c. are regarded as diphthongs and written simply *iə*, the length of the first elément being implied. as in *ei*; on the same principle *aeə* and *aoə* are simplified into *eə* and *oə*.)

II.

ə disp·yuut wəns ər·ouz bit wiin dhə wind ənd dhə sən, whic wəz dhə stroqgər əv dhə tuu, ənd dhei əg·riid tə put dhə point on ·dhis ishu, dhət whice·və suunist meid a

P

trævlə teik of iz klouk, shud bi ək auntid dhə moə
pauəfəl.   dhə wind big·æn, ənd bluu widh aol iz mait
ən mein ə blast, kould ən fiəs əz ə threishyən staom; bət
dhə stroqgə hii bluu dhə klousə dhə trævlə ræpt iz klouk
ər·aund im, ənd dhə taitə hii graspt it widh iz hændz.
dhen brouk aut dhə sən : widh iz welkəm biimz hii dis-
p·oest dhə veipər ən dhə kould ; dhə trævlə felt dhə jiinyəl
waomth, ənd əz dhə sən shon braitər ən braitə, hii sæt
daun, ouvək·əm widh dhə hiit, ənd kast hiz klouk on dhə
graund.

III.

it əp·iəz dhət dhər ar in iqglənd ən weilz, in raund
nəmbəz, faiv milyən culdrən əv dhə leibəriq popyəl eishən,
huu mei bi exp·ektid tu ət·end pəblik elim·entəri skuulz.
əb·aut haf dhis nəmbər ar æktyuəli on dhə roulz əv səc
skuulz.   wii mei estimeit dhət əb·aut haf-ə-m ilyən culdrən
ænyuəli pas dhə limit əv dhə skuul eij ənd entər on ə laif
əv leibə.   dhə haiist stændəd fixt in dhiiz skuulz, dhə
sixth stændəd, rik·waiəz dhə pyuupl tə riid ə shaot pæsij
frəm ə buk oə nyuuspeipə, ən tə rait ə shaot thiim widh
kər·ekt speliq—not ə veri hai rik waiəmənt soetnli.   hau
meni culdrən riict dhis stændəd ?   ounli twenti thauznd ;
whail dhə nəmbər əv tiicəz, ink·luudiq pyuupltiicəz, im-
p·loid iz əb·aut fifti thauznd ; dhæt iz, tuu pyuuplz pər
ænəm fər evri faiv tiicəz !   ounli əb·aut wən həndrəd
thauznd culdrən ænyuəli evə get biy·ond dhə thoed
stændəd, whic miinz dhə riidiq əv ən iizi staoribuk, ənd
raitiq ə shaot pæsij frəm dhə seim widh kər·ekt speliq.

ADDITIONAL NOTES.

§ **22**, p. 8. *French Nasals.* I now doubt the necessity of any guttural compression in the formation of the French nasals : their deep tone may be due simply to the greater lowering of the uvula than in South German and American nasality.

§ **28**, p. 10. *note* b. *Whispered Vowels.* Professor Storm says that whispered vowels are very common in the Malagasy language of Madagascar, as in the tribe-name ' Bets(i)m(i)sˑar(a)k(a),' where the whispered sounds are enclosed in parentheses [a]. 'Christ' in the Malagasy version is spelt 'Kraist,' but it ought consistently to have been written 'K(i)rais(i)t(ra),' as a native observed to Professor Storm.

§ **30**, p. 11. *Tongue Positions.* Bell's diagrams should be compared. In passing from (i) to (e) and (æ) successively, not only is the tongue lowered, but the point of greatest narrowness is also shifted further back, the size of the resonance-chamber in the front of the mouth being thus increased in both directions. Hence the ease with which (ạ) passes into (æ) by shifting the point of narrowness a little more forward. It is also clear that in forming (e) the passage may be made as narrow as for (i), without confounding the two sounds : the Danish (e¹) is, in fact, an (i) formed further in from the point of the tongue.

[a] The final (a) is almost, or entirely, silent, as pronounced by Professor Storm.

§ **58**, p. 23. *Acoustic Qualities of Vowels.* The Danish phonetician Jessen, for instance, goes so far as to entirely identify (*i*) with (e), (*e*) with (æ), &c., and consequently comes to the conclusion that 'close' and 'open' are purely relative terms, (*i*) and (e) being open as compared with (i), but close as compared with (*e*) and (æ).

§ **69**, p. 26. Professor Storm says that Russian 'jery' is certainly not nasal: as he pronounces it, it sounds to me simply as (ih), apparently with slight rounding.

§ **71**, p. 26. The German &c. (eh) in ' gabe ' may also be the wide (*e*h), although its indistinct glide-like character makes it difficult to identify with certainty. It seems to be quite distinct from the French sound in ' que.'

§ **87**, p. 29. The long Swedish *u* seems to a Norwegian ear to approximate to (yɪ).

§ **88**, p. 29. (*u*h) is better exemplified in the Norwegian than the Swedish pronunciation. The Swedish sound is, I believe, the English (*u*) formed with the lips in the low-round position.

§ **112**, p. 39. (ˌs) is not quite the Spanish sound, which has really something of a (th)-character, the blade position being modified by advancing the tip of the tongue, which does not touch the teeth.

§ **113**, p. 39. The Spanish soft *d*, according to Professor Storm, varies a good deal, being sometimes a very weak sound between (ˌz) and (dh), often being quite mute.

§ **117**, p. 41. The Spanish *b* is not simple (bh). See note to § 133 below.

§ **126**, p. 42. The English (w) may, as remarked in the text, be pronounced without raising the back of the tongue to the full (*u*) position, which would give consonantal (o^1) instead of (u). Professor Storm hears in French *loi*, *louer* the Norwegian (o^1) in 'kone.'

§ 129. p. 43. The Norwegian *sj* in ' sjæl' is, according to Professor Storm, identical with the Polish $ś=(shj)$. (sj) is Russian according to him.

§ 130, p. 44. The Slavonic barred *l* is, after all, probably (ɪ), and with secondary point-division$=(ɪ^*l)$, as stated independently by Bell and Storm.

§ 132, p. 44, note b. See note to § 244 below.

§ 133, p. 45. The lip-divided-voice seems, according to Professor Storm's pronunciation and analysis, to be the Spanish soft *b*. It might be written (b*l*).

§ 192, p. 62. I learn from Mr. Ellis that there is a very interesting distinction made between aspirated and unaspirated final breath-stops in some of the modern Indian languages, *akh* being pronounced like final (k) in English,$=$(ak[ʜ]), while in *ak* the off-glide is made inaudible by cessation of outgoing breath.

§ 222, p. 77. As (ta) develops into (tʜa) by throwing an independent stress on to the glide, so (da) becomes (dʌa) by emphasising the voice-glide. I have lately convinced myself by personal audition of the correctness of this (Mr. Ellis's) analysis of the Indian *dh* &c. in *dhanu*. Initially, of course, (t[ʌ]a)$=da$ develops into (tʌa).

§ 239, p. 82. In some cases there is not only no glide, but the consonants are even formed simultaneously. Thus 'open,' in my pronunciation, ends with an (m) and an (n) formed simultaneously, the lip-closure of the (p) being continued during the formation of the (n)—(oo^1pn*m).

§ 241, p. 83. In such glideless combinations as (kl) in English, the off-glide of the (k) is often heard as a devocalisation of the beginning of the (l), which might be

expressed by writing (k[lh]l). This makes it difficult
to distinguish between (tsh) and (t[jh]j) in such words as
'nature.'

§ **244**, p. 85. I have now, by the help of Professor
Storm's directions, acquired the 'thick' Norwegian *l*
(§ **132**, note b above). It is r↓ finished off with momentary contact of the tongue-tip and the inside of the
arch, the tongue moving forwards all the while, and
seems, therefore, to be a sort of inversion of the Japanese
r. The second element is quite instantaneous in its
formation, almost like a single strong trill. I would write
this sound (r↓[l↓]) rather than (r↓[d↓]), there being no
stoppage of the mouth passage, but only contact of the
tongue-tip. The effect is mainly that of (r) with a slight
(l) quality.

P. 110, l. 3. The vowel in 'bird' ought strictly to be
represented by *oe*, which I have adopted in the Appendix.

P. 111, l. 12. Add 'rather the Norwegian open *u*.'

P. 123. Professor Storm entirely repudiates most of the
values assigned by Bell to the French nasals, accepting
those first given, which represent my own analysis also.
He prefers (as I do now) (æq) to (æ*q*), and also (œq) to
(æh*q*).

P. 144. The Icelandic unaccented *u* in 'mönnum,'
'ríkur' seems to be generally simple (eh) or (*e*h), and the
i of 'ríki' seems to incline towards (*e*¹).

P. 146. (ᴋ) and (ɢ) ought to have been written (k*j*)
and (g*j*) consistently with § **149**.

P. 147. The notation (æ'gɪ) is the correct one, for the
on- as well as the off-glide seems to be really whispered.

P. 153. In Swedish Broad Romic 'daaga,' &c. might be
written simply 'daga,' the length of the vowel being taken

for granted before a single consonant. In the consonants the otherwise superfluous *z* might be used for (sh), as in ' zuta '=*skjuta* [a].

P. 154. I have since learnt that in natural Swedish pronunciation (r) before (t), (d), and (n) is slightly retracted, making the following consonants either half (ɟ) or else strongly (ɩ), it is difficult to decide which, and is itself reduced to a mere glide. These assimilations take place everywhere both after long and short vowels. Hence *våda* (danger), and *vårda* (to guard), are distinguished as (vvɔ¹ɪda) and (vvɔ¹ɪdɟa) [b].

P. 155. Professor Storm has heard this (ɒj) not only for soft *g*, but also for original (j), as in the song (ɒjɑɪ ɒjɑɪgvɪl vleɪva ɒjɑɪgvɪl dəɪ-i no¹ɪdɟehn) [c]. He also considers (ɽjh) to be the general pronunciation of soft *k*.

[a] As has been done by Swedish phoneticians themselves.

[b] These facts are generally acknowledged, I believe, by Swedish philologists. My study of Swedish pronunciation was, unfortunately, made in almost complete ignorance of their works.

[c] Yes, I will live, I will die in the North.

ERRATA.

§ 19, p. 7, ll. 4, 5, *for* ɔ *read* ɔ¹.

§ 43, p. 16, *under* (æh) *for* [oh] *read* [oh].

§ 80, p. 28, l. 3, *for* ại *read* ạɪ.

§ 90, p. 30, l. 2, *for* dotte *read* dot.

§ 113, p. 39, l. 2, *for* aa *read* a.

§ 236, p. 81, l. 2, *for* whisper *read* voice.

§ 279, p. 95, l. 5, *for* ⌿ \ ʌʌ *read* ⌿ \ vʌ.

§ 301, p. 102, *note* b, *for* (e) *read* (i).

§ 307, p. 105, l. 5, *for* a= *read* a=.

P. 123, l. 18, *for* œhq *read* œq.

P. 124, l. 7, *for* dotte *read* dot.

P. 134, l. 17, *for* ʌ *read* [ʌ].

P. 156, l. 2 (Sentences), *omit the* v *before* veɪdrreht *and* vakkehrt.

Made in United States
North Haven, CT
15 June 2022